Northumberland & Cumberland Mining Disasters

Other Titles in the Series

Durham Mining Disasters c.1700–1950s
Maureen Anderson – ISBN 1 845630 73 4

Lancashire Mining Disasters 1835–1910
Jack Nadin – ISBN 1 903425 95 6

South Yorkshire Mining Disasters Vol 1: The Nineteenth Century
Brian Elliott – ISBN 1 903425 64 6

Pits and Pitmen of Barnsley
Brian Elliott – ISBN 1 903425 03 04

The Miners' Strike Day By Day
Brian Elliott & Arthur Wakefield – ISBN 1 903425 58 1

Yorkshire's Flying Pickets in the 1884/85 Miners' Strike
Brian Elliott & Bruce Wilson – ISBN 1 903425 16 6

Yorkshire Mining Veterans
Brian Elliott – ISBN 1 903425 16 6

Pits: A Pictorial Record of Mining
John Threlkeld – ISBN 1 903425 58 1

Lord Mason. Barnsley Pitman to Peer.
An Illustrated Biography
Brian Elliot – ISBN 978 1 84563 036 2

Northumberland & Cumberland Mining Disasters

MAUREEN ANDERSON

MINING HERITAGE
SERIES

Series Editor

Brian Elliott

Wharncliffe Books

First published in Great Britain in 2009 by
Wharncliffe Books
an imprint of
Pen & Sword Books Ltd
47 Church Street
Barnsley
South Yorkshire
S70 2AS

Copyright © Maureen Anderson 2009

ISBN 978-1-84563-081-2

Typeset in 10pt Palatino by
Mac Style, Beverley, East Yorkshire

Printed and bound in the UK by
CPI

Pen & Sword Books Ltd incorporates the Imprints of Pen & Sword Aviation, Pen & Sword Maritime, Pen & Sword Military, Wharncliffe Local History, Pen and Sword Select, Pen and Sword Military Classics and Leo Cooper.

For a complete list of Pen & Sword titles please contact
PEN & SWORD BOOKS LIMITED
47 Church Street, Barnsley, South Yorkshire, S70 2AS, England
E-mail: enquiries@pen-and-sword.co.uk
Website: www.pen-and-sword.co.uk

Contents

Acknowledgements

The working coal mines of Britain are now becoming a distant memory along with the haunting echoes of weeping widows and children. For supplying information and images to assist in the compilation of this work, which I hope serves as a reminder of the enormous human sacrifice of those who laboured in often appalling conditions and for the part they played in creating our industrial and social history, I am sincerely grateful. As always Brian Elliott, my editor, has given me the benefit of his experience by offering suggestions and support throughout the project's process. I would like to thank Wharncliffe/Pen and Sword Books for giving me the opportunity to write this volume. A special thanks to Ian Winstanley for passing on to me the invaluable notes he has amassed over the years. The Durham Mining Museum (www.dmm.org.uk) and the Haig Mining Museum (www.haigpit.com) play an invaluable role in collating and preserving data and images on all aspects of mining in their respective areas and I am indebted to them for their assistance. Thank you also to George Nairn for the use of postcards from his superb collection and to Dimity Pollard (Australia) for the images of her ancestors William and Margaret Shields. As always I owe thanks to the ever helpful and friendly staff of Hartlepool Reference Library and finally to my husband, Jim, for trekking around the country with me in my quest for information.

Introduction

In the early years of coal mining numerous pits had been sunk with the areas worked being shallow and of no great extent. Water and chokedamp would have caused problems but the presence of firedamp was minimal, although records show that it did cause accidents on a few occasions. As the demand for coal increased the pits became deeper and worked over a larger area, branching away from a single shaft. These extensive workings were harder to ventilate adequately and the single shaft meant there was only one way in and out. To work these larger pits more people were employed so there was a greater chance of multiple fatalities.

In the nineteenth century explosions were the most common cause of deaths underground. Pockets of inflammable gas built up and, if not discovered, would ignite at a naked light. When safety lamps were introduced they were originally only used in 'fiery mines' but even if they were available hewers preferred to work with candles as they gave off a much better light. Inundations of water also took a heavy toll on life. Included in this volume are some accidents which would not statistically be recorded as a disaster but they demonstrate the variety of dangers that were present everyday of a pit-worker's life.

In the nineteenth century rescue attempts after an accident were haphazard affairs with those on the surface only being able to guess at what destruction had taken place below ground. Because of the effects of afterdamp time was of the essence in getting trapped workers to the surface. There was such a strong bond between the people of the mining communities that often heroic, and sometimes foolhardy, efforts would result in the rescuers themselves losing their lives. Until trained teams were established in the early twentieth century those that descended the pit with the object of rescue would have little or no medical knowledge so would have only been able to assist the injured in a very minor capacity and would probably often have caused more pain or even death by moving or lifting the victim in the wrong way. Those who had suffered broken bones, wounds and burns must have suffered excruciating pain as they were transported along the underground roadways and up the shaft. When a survivor (or a body) was recovered from the pit anything that was available would be used to take him to his home. This could be a cart or a barrow usually filled with straw or old coats. In miners' homes there would be no facilities for proper treatment of the injured so a doctor and the family would just do the best they could.

The earlier disasters were recorded in very little detail as most of the coal-owners, with seemingly little regard for the lives of their workforce, would have wanted the public to be kept in ignorance as to the number of injuries and deaths that took place within the pits, fearing that pressure would have been exerted on them to put costly safety measures in place and to provide for the families of the victims. This extract by Sykes from *The Evidence into the State of the Coal Trade*, published in 1835, explains the situation:

Explosions and other Casualties happened as frequently in our collieries formerly as at the present time; but the servility of the local press prevented their being given to the public. The following extract from the *Newcastle Journal* of March 21st 1767, will prove this assertion:

'So many deplorable accidents have lately happened in collieries, it certainly claims the attention of coal-owners to make a provision for the distressed widows and fatherless children occasioned by these mines, as the catastrophe from foul air becomes more common than ever, as we have been requested to take no notice of these things, which in fact could have very little good tendency, we drop the farther mentioning of it; but before we dismiss the subject, as a laudable example for their imitation, we recommend the provision made in the Trinity House for distressed seaman, seaman's widows etc., which in every respect is praiseworthy, and confers honour on that brotherhood.'

Sykes then adds:

From this it is reasonable to conclude, that there must have, at that time, have been a dreadful sweep of human life in one or more of the neighbouring collieries; and it is from such injunctions laid upon the newspaper editors, that these occurrences for a great number of years were kept as much as possible from the public.

Prior to 1814, few inquests were held on pit-workers killed underground, so accurate numbers of either multiple or singular fatalities are unknown. In most cases the only records that survive of the dangers in the early pits are those recorded by early historians such as Sykes and Fordyce in their *Local Records*, Galloway in his *Annals of Coal Mining* and Richardson in his *Borderer's Table*. Parish burial registers occasionally supply names and dates such as the following from St Andrew's, Newcastle:

April 24th 1695, were buried James Archer and his son Stephen who in the month of May 1658 were drowned in a coal pitt in the Galla Flat by the breaking in of water from an old waste. The bodys were found intire after they had lyen in the water 36 years and 11 months.

The majority of inquests concluded with a verdict of accidental death, often with one of the victims being blamed. The coal owners were rich and influential so those men that acted as jurors and the press would be loath to lay blame at their door. The first in-depth account of multiple fatalities that was aired to the public by means of the newspapers was on the explosion at Felling in 1812 when ninety-one men and boys perished. By 1842 an invaluable record in the form of accounts accompanied by images came into being when the *Illustrated London News* was first published. The text would sometimes sensationalise the facts of the event and the lists of the victims were often inaccurate but the drawings of the commercially-trained artists of all aspects of mining and its perils were as visually dramatic as any later photographic record. Other publications, such as *The Graphic* (from 1870), followed the example of using images to enhance the stories. From the early twentieth century photographic images of the aftermath of a disaster were often made into postcards and sold as souvenirs. On occasions these were made up of a collage of smaller photos depicting both victims and survivors, leaving us with a good visual source of research for family historians.

The victims of early mining accidents often left behind very large families without any means of support with the only possibility of any income at all coming from other branches of the family or donations from the public. If a widow did not have children of an age capable of working in the pit she would be evicted from her house and for many this would have meant the only option would have been the workhouse.

Historical records, gravestones and memorials show us the appalling number of deaths of young children in the pits. The extreme poverty that the families within the mining communities suffered meant that an extra wage, however small, eased the financial burden. There are records of parents begging officials to employ their children, sometimes even adding a year or two to their correct age. These children, sometimes as young as four or five, would sit or crouch in almost complete darkness for anything up to sixteen hours a day opening and shutting the trap doors that controlled the ventilation. This resulted in lasting deformities such as crooked backs or bandy legs. Often they would be carried to the pit still asleep on the backs of their fathers and taken home again in the same manner. The coal-owners preferred to employ children as they were cheaper. A grown man would not work for the wage that was offered and also would consider the work beneath him. Little wonder that there are instances of children falling asleep at their post and neglecting their door causing a build up of gas and ultimately an explosion. J B Atkinson, a mines inspector, however, did point out that on one occasion where an explosion in a Durham coal-pit was attributed to a child's neglect every door had been blown out in the blast so how, he asked, could the cause have been substantiated? As children grew older they would move on to other tasks, sometimes beyond their physical capacity, and injuries, often severe, were commonplace.

Inaccuracy of names and ages of victims was common, even on some memorials, as illiteracy on the part of the families, poorly written records and a lack of knowledge as to the year of birth produced discrepancies. Wherever possible the names and ages listed in these chapters have been checked against every available source to keep errors to a minimum.

Northumberland was part of the Great Northern Coal Field with pits from the borders of County Durham to Scotland while Cumberland's mining activity was concentrated on the west coast of the county – with some of the workings stretching for miles under the seabed. These vast underground tunnels became a source of amazement for tourists of the nineteenth century.

Coal mining was a huge part of our industrial heritage and was the formation of many of the towns that now look elsewhere for their income. Sadly the wealth of a few was accumulated on the blood of many of those who worked in these dank, dark, uncomfortable and dangerous underground workplaces, pulling the valuable black commodity from the bowels of the earth. This heritage came at a cost which for thousands of our forbears was far too high, with thousands killed or maimed in often avoidable 'accidents'. Many of the victims of the coal mines are commemorated on memorials but countless others lie in unmarked graves, their tragic end almost obliterated by the passage of time. It is to be hoped by including every recorded disaster in Northumberland and Cumberland, in a small way, this publication will serve as a reminder of a time when many children never reached their teens and others were left fatherless; wives became widows in the blink of an eye; and the heroes had to remove the mutilated bodies of a member of their family, a friend or a neighbour from the underground site of their death or perhaps watch them linger in unimaginable agony.

Part One

Brief Accounts of Multiple Fatalities
from 1710

The *Borderer's Table Book* includes this rather vague entry for 1710:

> About this year Bensham colliery exploded, by which lamentable catastrophe, between seventy and eighty human beings lost their lives. At this colliery the first attempt was made to work the low main seam of coal in the neighbourhood of Newcastle.

Although it is fairly certain there would have been other fatal accidents during the years following the date of this report the next disaster to be recorded was on 5 August 1737 when twenty-two persons were killed in an explosion at Corpshill (or Corporal) Pit in Cumberland. In the pay-bill for that month there was the following entry:

> Firedamp killed 22 at 4 o'clock in ye M. £8 3s 10d for searching for and taking up 22 dead (persons) and three horses, mending thirls, etc after the Great Fire Damp.

The coal-owner, Sir James Lowther, immediately ordered that £100 be distributed amongst the families of the victims.

Hartley Colliery as sketched by Thomas H Hair in 1844. An explosion here in 1761 claimed five lives. Author's collection

As an explosion took place it often forced smoke, flames and debris to erupt from the pit as if shot from the mouth of a cannon. Author's collection

Grieving families and friends attempt to console each other as they await news following a pit accident. Author's collection

Hartley Colliery was situated about nine miles NNE of Newcastle-upon-Tyne. In *Local Records* John Sykes states only that on 1 December 1761 an explosion took place in which Mr Curry, the viewer, and four others lost their lives. On 24 November 1834 the shaft rope broke sending four men and a boy plummeting to their deaths. The men, Thomas Martin, William Witty and John Barrick, left three widows and ten children between them.

Little appears to be known on the beginnings of Walker Colliery other than the coal was leased by a company from Newcastle Corporation around 1758 and opened prior to 1765 when it was sunk to a depth of about 100 fathoms. On Monday, 1 April 1765 the pit fired with no loss of life but the workers suffered severe burns and were transported to the infirmary. On the following day several overmen and others descended the shaft to assess the damage when there was a second explosion which killed eight men and seventeen horses 'who were all burnt in a most shocking manner'. On Tuesday, 18 March 1766 another explosion at the same pit took a further ten lives.

Wallsend Colliery, also known as Russell's Wallsend, appears to have been first sunk in about 1780 by William Russell and his family. There were several pits including the Church or C Pit which was named for its close proximity to the parish church. A railway line carried waggons of coal down an incline 'by the hand of a single individual'. A railway from another colliery crossed this line on a wooden bridge. The shaft-frame that supported the pulleys was made of wood and on the wheels were ropes that lowered men and materials. There was a tall brick funnel on top of the upcast shaft and a railed platform near the top to facilitate repairs. An engine house contained the machinery for working the ropes and situated nearby were the boilers which raised the steam that powered the pit. The mine had a four inch metal pipe which was used to conduct the firedamp from the bottom of the pit to be burned off at the top. Generally this discharge of gas from the coal was slow and imperceptible; but when met with in the shape of blowers issuing from small fissures in the face of the coal and chinks in the roof could rush into the workings with some violence and there would be a noise like the letting off of steam. Usually this could be ignored but occasionally there would be a large enough quantity of gas to cause an explosion. It was recorded that the pitmen had been known to collect the gas in clay bottles and burn them at home for light by making a small hole in the clay. Although eventually becoming extremely profitable, Wallsend was the scene of many fatalities. In October 1782, gas ignited at a candle of a hewer. Presumably in fear of his life, the man ran away without trying to extinguish the flames and it was left to the overman to do so. Before he could reach the source he was overcome by the smoke and noxious gases and suffocated. The pit then had to be flooded to extinguish the burning coal and brattice. In November and December of 1784, there were two explosions taking the lives of three men in the former and two in the latter with none of the bodies being recovered for several months. The firing was supposedly caused by the spark from a steel mill being used by men working in the shaft. This was strongly disputed at the time as it was not thought that steel mills could cause ignition but this belief was refuted in the following year. In the repairs which followed these

An illustration showing rescuers finding a group of bodies after an explosion. Author's collection

In a scene all too common families and friends rush to a pit after an explosion. Author's collection

explosions a carpenter was employed immediately above the mouth of the shaft. As he was using his bright and shiny new saw it caught the rays of the sun which mirrored the light to the bottom of the shaft. This caused terror to those below who thought the pit had fired. It was then realized that using a mirror to throw the sun's light in this manner could be used when no other form of light was available.

Further explosions at this colliery occurred on 9 June 1785 (one man killed) and on 4 December (two killed). The former accident was ascertained to have been ignited by the

A sketch of the drops at Wallsend by Thomas H Hair in 1844. This was one of the early methods used for loading the coal onto the waiting vessels. Author's collection

spark of a steel mill as John Selkirk survived the accident and was able to report on the event. On the afternoon of 9 April 1786, most of the men and boys had left the pit but the back overman, one hewer and four trappers were still underground when the pit fired. One of the trappers, a little boy, was taken out alive but died of his injuries soon after. The explosion occurred as the overman was drawing props when there was a fall of roof which released gas which ignited at an open light. The six victims were Charles and Joseph Dodds, James Patterson, Ralph Dixon, Matthew Elliott and Mark Maddison. Following the accident the practice was changed and no props were withdrawn when the pit was working. The last explosion in the eighteenth century to take multiple victims at Wallsend was on Monday, 4 October 1790 when the following seven men and boys were killed: Joseph Wilson, aged 13; John Lee (14); Thomas Holmes (18); Christopher Barras (20); Thomas Birbeck (20); Thomas Morrow (30); and John Ward (37).

In 1791, an inundation took place in one of the Whitehaven mines caused by water breaking through from old workings. Two men, a woman and five horses were drowned. With the release of the water the old workings collapsed causing subsidence on the surface and considerable damage to buildings in the vicinity.

Wallsend continued to be a dangerous pit in the nineteenth century. On Tuesday, 20 September 1803, at C Pit, at least thirteen men and boys were killed when a burst of gas or 'bag of foulness' (which came from the roof in the pillars behind the workmen) fired at a lamp in the leading excavation. The workings were very dry and dusty which caused the fire from the explosion to sweep along the bords and strike all the workers within its range.

Church Pit at Wallsend Colliery which was plagued by fatal accidents in the eighteenth century. The image is from an etching by Thomas H Hair. Author's collection

There were about twenty men and boys who were furthest from the blast and these were showered with red-hot sparks from the ignited dust. Most of the victims died immediately from suffocation but it is probable that some of those who were burnt would also not have survived. Eleven of the thirteen or more victims were named as Matthew Fogget (aged 14); George Fogget (age unknown); Thomas Parkin (14); Nicholas Raw (16); John Revely (16); Cuthbert Rumford (16); Anthony Parkin (18); Ralph Dawson (22); John Hann (22); Jonas Hammon (?); and William Kelly (?).

Thomas Hair wrote that a coal mine near Benwell took fire by a candle and burned for nearly thirty years. It acquired such great strength that it travelled about a mile from the source and under the Fenham grounds where it erupted in nearly twenty places throwing out sulphur and red hot ashes. Hair puts the year of this event at around 1684. During the seventeenth century the pit was sunk to the Low Main Seam. The seam was carried under the haugh at the west of what became the village of Paradise and, during a severe flood around the 1650s, water broke through the workings. The water was eventually drawn out and the seam completed and worked until near the end of that century. The pit then lay dormant until 1789 when a new seam was sunk to the depth of sixty fathoms (360 feet). Richard Fynes records that at the Paradise (or W Pit) at Benwell eleven perished on Friday, 24 April 1795. There are no further details on the accident but Fynes' date may be wrong or this may have been two separate accidents as the local parish register lists the following eight as pitmen buried in March of that year:

Buried 25 March 1795; James, son of James Anderson; Thomas, son of Thomas Dance; Joseph, son of Edward Towns; Thomas, son of Thomas Aaronfield; Joseph Proctor.

Buried 26 March 1795; John, son of John Cram.

Buried 28 March 1795; Jonas, son of Jonas Stringer.

Buried 29 March 1795; Thomas, son of William Morland.

An entry in *Local Records* states that in September 1796 'by the pricking of an old waste at Slaty Ford in Northumberland six persons unfortunately lost their lives'.

Benwell Staiths as sketched by Thomas H Hair in 1844. Author's collection

Female coal-bearers carry their load up the steep incline. Author's collection

In the early nineteenth century details were still very sparse on some disasters with only a mention of an explosion at a Whitehaven pit in 1806 which claimed eleven lives and another that took place at the Wellington Pit at Walbottle near Newcastle on 28 April 1816 when either thirteen or fourteen lives were lost. According to Galloway's *Annals of Coal Mining and the Coal Trade*:

An explosion raged with terrific fury through the excavations to a distance of two hundred yards in one continued flame. The workmen made their escape by the Blucher pit, except thirteen who were dreadfully bruised or scorched.

The *Borderer's Table* book records that there were 120 men and boys working in the pit at the time of the accident and 'three men and eleven boys were dreadfully scorched'.

The pit-workers leaving the pit at the end of their shift. An image published in the Harper's Weekly. www.chmrc.co.uk

17

Part Two

The Pit Children

1806–1841

Is a half-marrow, has been so this two months; has been down this pit 4 years. The high pit; very often, nearly every day, rubbed the skin off his back. The places are heavy. Mostly puts the full corf up-hill; very often strains himself when the corf sticks against the roof and the side-props. Is working all in the broken. The bad air hurts him so that he cannot speak sometimes. Got lamed in his hand today by a fall of stone which killed his marrow, William Bruce, who was 16 years old. Another boy was cut in the head. One got his foot lamed by the rolleys and was off a week; was also off a week by his hand being hurt by a horse. The fall of stone today happened just after the corf passed the spot; the corf had stuck against the timber-props and stood a minute or two, then they shoved on to come away: does not think the stone was properly propped up. Can read (fairly) can write his name. Goes to Sunday-school and chapel very often. (Has arm in a sling and looks very pale the effects of the accident mentioned.) Has three brothers down the pit, one a headsman, another a driver and the third a helper-up.

James Long, aged 16, Hartley, 1841

Before shaft cages came into general use the pit-workers would descend in a tub or by rope as the illustration shows. Accidents were common as fatigue, especially in children, often caused loss of grip. Author's collection

The plight of the children who worked in the factories had their lot improved slightly when legislature was introduced in 1802 curtailing working hours and forcing the employers to allow schooling. In 1833, new regulation in the form of the Factories Act brought further improvements but the Act did not extend to children in coalmines. The apathy of genteel Victorian society, especially towards industry in the North, was perhaps not altogether a lack of caring but more of ignorance. To the population that lived in the south little was known about northerners other than they were a strange breed with a language of their own. Also those involved in the financial benefits of the industry fought long and hard to keep the sordid details of how the coal was won from the general public. Coal was a very necessary commodity and to look beyond the flickering flames of their cosy fires or the smoke that came from their factory chimneys which manufactured the goods they craved was of no interest to the Victorians.

As with any cause there were a handful of reformers but it was not until the explosion at St Hilda's in 1835 that the campaign was stepped up and society was shaken from its apathy. Eventually the objections of the coal-owners were drowned out when the results of investigations into the employment of children in mines were completed. There were no females working below ground in Durham or Northumberland but they were employed in other coalfields, including Cumberland. The report by the Royal Commission resulted in legislature being introduced in 1842 banning all females and all children under the age of ten being employed below ground at the collieries. Although still not enough, it was a step in the right direction.

(1) Pit: Killingworth

Location: Killingworth, Northumberland
Type: Explosion
Fatalities: 10
Date: Friday, 28 March 1806

Has just been down a week. Keeps a door. (George Kendall works besides him and states that he is very frightened when his low [candle] goes out and cries out. Is 12 hours down the pit and works in the night shift now) Cannot read or write. Was at school a short time. Goes in about a mile by.
William Simpson, aged 6, Killingworth, 1841

Drives a cuddy, and helps up now and then. Has been down the pit a year. Goes in above a mile by. (The cuddies, it is said, are hard to drive, and their drivers are on their legs nearly all the 12 hours.) Has been at school, night and day schools 2 years and reads very easy words. Goes to Sunday-school, and night-school, and chapel.
Robert Thwaites, aged about nine, Killingworth, 1841

Has been down pits 5 years. Drives a cuddy, and helps up. Gets about 1s 8d a day. These are the wages of a foal, for which he is bound. Always was very white and thin looking. Looks very much so now. Once was off 16 weeks by the rolleys running over his foot and arm and shoulder. Nothing was broken. Reads very easy words only. Cannot write. Goes to Sunday-school and chapel.
William Duffell, aged about 13, Killingworth, 1841

An etching of the village of Killingworth as it was in 1804.
Author's collection

Throughout the nineteenth century Killingworth was to be the scene of five disasters taking five lives or more. The youngest recorded deaths were of boys aged just eleven.

The first disaster of the century was caused by an explosion in March 1806. In the evidence taken at the inquest it was reported that the ventilation had decreased due to the upcast shaft being wet which had caused gas to collect. The gas had been discovered and the men were instructed to work with safety lamps with the naked lights being left at a nearby door. It appeared that a miner, strictly against orders, had taken gunpowder and candles into the workings which was considered to have been the cause of the ignition. The record of this disaster comes primarily from the account related nearly thirty years later in 1835 to the Select Committee on Accidents in Mines by George Stevenson, a witness, who had been working as an engineman at the colliery at the time of the explosion. When asked what he remembered he stated that the pit fired just after midday when most of the workers had left, otherwise the loss of life would have been far greater. Stevenson had sent four men down to prepare a place for a furnace and a fifth, an underlooker, had followed to oversee the work. Just as the last man descended there was a tremendous noise and thick smoke and debris, including stones and trusses of hay, shot up from the mouth of the pit. Stevenson thought that the hay, which had been sent down earlier that day, may have 'injured' the ventilation. The ground was trembling and cracking and the large pumps were displaced so the engines could not be worked. No one dared go near the shaft for some time but eventually, when the debris settled, a rope was lowered so that anyone at the bottom of the shaft could be hauled up. Several men who had been working in the adjoining pit were got out safely. As one man was being drawn up there was another, smaller, explosion which aided his ascent by pushing him upwards. Explosions continued over a period of two days and eventually fire engines were brought in from Newcastle to drown the workings in order to extinguish the fire. Stevenson estimated the cost had been £20,000 independent of the loss of life.

Of the five men who had been last to descend the pit four were found buried beneath some corves at the bottom of the shaft but the underlooker had managed to throw himself behind some pillars and although nearly all his clothes were burned from his body he had escaped with his life. It was to be four months before all the bodies were finally recovered.

The following eight names are recorded as 'lost at Killingworth Colliery on 28 March' in the burial register of St Bartholomew's church, Longbenton:

James Jobbs, pitman, aged 56, buried 9 July.
Robert Curry, pitman, aged 60, buried 17 July.
William Reed, pitman, aged 37, buried 19 July.
William Taylor, pitman, aged 40, buried 23 July.
William Mood, pitman, aged 44, buried 23 July.
James Brown, blacksmith, aged 19, buried 28 August.
Edward Wales, pitman, aged 22, buried 29 August.
William Brown, pitman, aged 34, buried 2 September.

The inquest found that the deaths were accidental, having been caused by gunpowder and candles being taken into the workings against the orders of the colliery officials.

On Thursday, 14 September 1809 another explosion occurred at Killingworth. The firedamp did not reach the shaft but twelve men lost their lives by suffocation from the afterdamp. Ten of the victims were buried on 15 and 16 September, also at St Bartholomew at Longbenton, with the burial register marked 'pitmen killed 14 September':

James Cook, aged 18; Robert Wheeler, aged18; James Davison, aged 23; George Gildroy, aged 27; John Gildroy, aged 42; William Scott, aged 31; Moses Stewart, aged 32; Robert Hall, aged 34; John Burrel, aged 39; John Mason, aged 50.

(2) Pit: Heaton Main

Location: Heaton, Northumberland
Type: Inundation
Fatalities: 75
Date: Wednesday, 3 May 1815

Has been down pits more than a year. Drives now. Was well in his breath before he went down the pit. Is now very short of breath and is bad about the breast. Never feels any other pain. The doctor puts a blister on. Has been off work 6 weeks. Is near the shaft in the pit. His work is not very hard. The air of the pit does not agree with him. Feels his breath short soon after he goes down the pit. Feels it nearly all day, not after he comes up. No one strikes him.

Saunders Blackburn, aged 9, Heaton, 1841.

Heaton Main Colliery had severe problems from its beginnings, partly because it was worked to a depth of 500 feet, which was very deep for those times, and partly because it was a wet seam with numerous faults; and descending on a 1 in 10 gradient. Within close proximity was the Heaton Banks Colliery that had closed in 1745 which, it was suspected, was now a vast underground reservoir. Between 1813 and 1814 there had been three near misses with water seeping into the current works but with the pit nearing exhaustion, ignoring the warnings of engineers of the possible danger, the owners pressed on to harvest the remaining high grade coal. In the last week of April 1815 John Buddle, head viewer, noticed 'a small bleeding of water from the coal' and advised that care should be taken. A barrier of coal remained between the disused pit and the Stable Drift and boreholes were made to ascertain when they were near the old waste and then plugged when water came from them. A few days later there was 'a greater bleeding of water' but no precautions were taken. At 4am on 3 May Mr Miller, the underviewer, descended the pit to inspect the area where water dripping heavily from the roof had been brought to his attention. He decided he would send in borers to ascertain where the water was coming from. About fifteen minutes later two of the drifters became extremely alarmed as the water started running more freely so they sent a boy to warn those working nearby. The boy, probably terrified, did not carry out his orders and instead ran for the shaft and safety. The two drifters then heard a crash and immediately afterwards a gust of wind extinguished their candles which prompted them to leave with haste. They fled towards the shaft, which was about a mile from where they had been working, reaching safety just prior to the deluge. Seventeen others, some wading through waist deep water, also managed to escape. It was about 5am when the coalface had fractured and thousands of gallons of water poured in. Following a natural course, the fast moving tide flowed to the lower parts of the pit, closing off the bottom of the shaft and thereby cutting off the only means of escape.

Three large engines were employed in endeavouring to remove the water from the shaft but it was rising faster than it could be pumped out. By Wednesday evening the water in the shaft had reached nineteen fathoms and by the following afternoon this had increased to thirty. On Friday morning, some distance away, seven large chasms opened up in the ground which confirmed the suspicions that the old workings had been a reservoir. As the water had flowed into Heaton Main the levels in the old waste had gone down causing the ground above to collapse. No one living in the vicinity had previously known of the existence of these parts of the old workings of the Heaton Bank Colliery. In the first month following the disaster it was calculated that over 50 million gallons of water were drawn from the pit and the draining continued for a considerable time after.

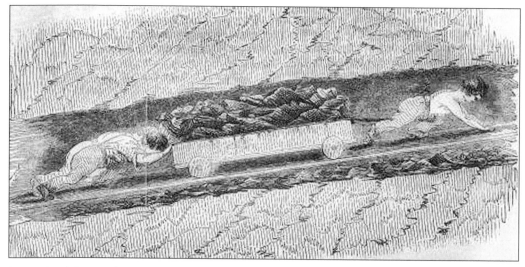

Young boys drag and push a rolley loaded with coal up a steep incline. www.chmrc.co.uk

An account of the events taken from local papers and the *Gentleman's Magazine* was recorded in *The Borderer's Table* of which this is an extract:

Every possibility of retreat to those left behind was now cut off; and seventy-five human beings (forty-one men and thirty-four boys), including Mr Miller, were shut up in the workings towards the rise of the colliery, either to perish by hunger, or to die for want of respirable air. The sufferers who thus found a living grave, left twenty-four widows and seventy-seven children, besides Mrs Miller, and her eight children, to deplore their untimely fate.

On the 6th of January 1816, the first human body of the sufferers was brought to bank, in a state of great decay, but ascertained, by the neck cloth, to be that of William Scott, between 70 and 80 years of age, who attended one of the furnaces. Of a knife which the deceased had in his pocket, the haft only (of bone) was entire, the blade being entirely corroded by the mixture of the pyrites in the mine with the water. His watch was also nearly destroyed by the same cause. It may, however, afford some speculation to the curious, that the articles of linen on the deceased were quite fresh and uninjured, but those of woollen fabric entirely destroyed. In a few weeks afterwards, the remains of the rest of these unfortunate men were found in different situations in the workings of the pit. February 20th, thirty-nine of the bodies, forming a melancholy procession, were interred in trenches in the south-east corner of Wallsend churchyard. Many of the bodies, when found, were nearly naked, and all in a state of great decay. They appeared to have all perished by starvation. They had got into a part of the pit where the water did not reach them, and had been many weeks employed in endeavouring to work their way into an old pit, by which they might have escaped. They are supposed to have failed in their attempt by the want of food to support them, as every horse in the pit was eaten to the bone.

Although this latter statement cannot be positively discounted it is highly unlikely that the trapped victims survived long enough to eat the horses as there would have been no fresh air and they would have been in total darkness.

From the *Liverpool Mercury* 16 June 1815:

All hopes of saving any of the poor workmen in Heaton Colliery must now be abandoned for the water drawn by the engines for these last few days has emitted an offensive and putrid smell, which leaves no doubt of the state of the bodies underground. If any circumstances can add to the agonised feelings of the poor widows and children, or augment the horrors of their situation, it is the water that unavoidably flows past many houses they now inhabit at the colliery.

With the information the coal-owners had been given as to the suspicion of the state of the old workings it could be deduced that this was a foreseeable tragedy but the inquest concluded that the inundation had been an accident.

The exact number of lives lost is uncertain as John Buddle calculated seventy-five, but his deputy, Matthias Dunn, wrote in 1848 that there were nearer to ninety. It was reported that of those lost there were six boys aged seven or under but only three names corresponding to those ages have been traced. Twenty-eight women were deprived of a husband and eighty-five children of a father. Sixty-six of the victims were buried in

John Buddle, head viewer at Heaton Main in 1815.
Author's collection

unmarked graves at St Peter's at Wallsend. In 1852, seventy-five trees were planted at Heaton Spinney to commemorate those that perished. The names of seventy-one of the victims have been found as follows:

Buried at Longbenton:
Nicholas Gibson (aged 18)
Edward Gibson (20)
Matthew Gibson (22)
Henry Widdington (20)
Ralph Widdington, junior (28)
Ralph Widdington, senior (56)
Shipley Mitchinson (42)

Buried at Wallsend:
Thomas Dodd (7)
William Graham (7)
William Elliott (7)
John Pratt (10)
Thomas Watson (10)
John Watson (12)
Thomas Gray (12)
Robert Southern (14)
Anthony Southern (18)
William Southern (25)
Christopher Grey (14)

Michael Wilson (15)
Nicholas Miller (15)
Thomas Gordon (15)
Jacob Curtis (15)
Ralph Hall (15)
William Gardner (15)
Thomas Gardner (17)
Jasper Gardner (24)
Thomas Miller (16)
James Dodd, junior (16)
James Dodd, senior (40)
William King (16)
Thomas Thompson (16)
Walter Stokoe, junior (17)
Walter Stokoe, senior (42)
Robert Lumsden (18)
John Gordon (19)
William Thew (17)
George Thew (20)
John Thew (50)
John Watson (20)

Charles Gardiner (20)
William Dixon (21)
William Thompson (21)
John Frame (21)
William Scott (21)
William Hall (21)
John Redhead (22)
William Renwick (23)
John Renwick (25)
Robert Steel (25)
George Steel (25)
John Reay (26)
Arthur Dixon, junior (26)
Arthur Dixon, senior (64)
Matthew Johnson (28)
Lancelot Nicholson (29)

John Gibson (31)
Robert Campbell (31)
Edward Robson (34)
George Dawson (36)
Simon Dodds (36)
Robert English (36)
John Newbill (37)
Andrew Brayson (40)
Henry Dixon (40)
Richard Gibson (45)
David Urwin (48)
George Laws (50)
Robert Richardson (64)
Edward Gibson (82)
William Green
John Robinson

One of those who escaped was Johnny Thew but his father and two older brothers, William and George, were to die in the pit. When William's body was recovered in his pocket was his candle-box on which he, with the certain knowledge that death was hovering close by, had used a nail to engrave a message to his mother. Although this widow, as did many others, managed to survive on subscriptions for a period of time eventually the money would become depleted and she would have had to depend on her own labour for a means of support. A few years after the disaster a Reverend Leigh Richmond was on a bible tour in the north when he heard the heart-rending story of the message left for Elizabeth Thew so, through a third party, asked if he could borrow the box on which the message had been written. It was lent to him on the condition that if any contributions were made because of his telling the story and exhibiting the box the money was to go to the widow. Eventually a sum of £16 10s was remitted to her. On Richmond's death Mrs Thew requested that the box be returned to her which was done. In about 1834 a travelling agent of the Sunday School Union of London, JR Wilson, borrowed the box on a similar understanding. Over three years a sum of £115 7s 3d was raised and paid to Mrs Thew at the rate of 5s a week and about £2 annual rent for a period of seven years. At the end of 1840 the funds were depleted and, at the age of sixty-eight and unable to work, the widow was destitute. She applied to the Gateshead Union and was allotted 2s a week but this was insufficient to pay her rent and keep her in food. An enterprising scheme was thought of to raise money for Mrs Thew and to bring to the attention of the public a reminder of the disaster. A pamphlet was printed in 1841 at the office of the *Great Northern Advertiser* and distributed to booksellers to be sold. The small publication related the story of the tragedy and the message of a boy to his mother from beyond the grave. An extract read as follows:

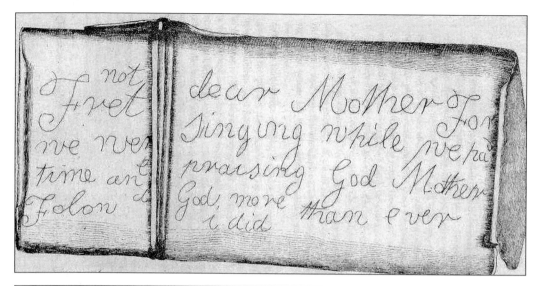

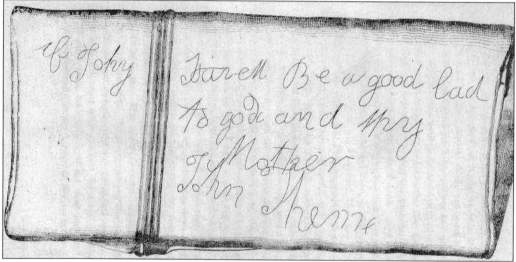

A facsimile of the message scratched on a candle box by William Thew as he and his comrades awaited certain death when they were trapped in Heaton Main Pit in 1815. Author's collection

MEMOIR OF WILLIAM THEW, ONE OF THE SUFFERERS IN THE INUNDATION OF HEATON COLLIERY, 1815:

William Thew was the second son of John and Elizabeth Thew, and was seventeen years of age at the time of the catastrophe. His father, and an elder brother, aged twenty, named George, perished with him. A younger brother, John, was one of those who, on the alarm of the bursting in of the water being made, escaped with others by the shaft. William and John were scholars in the Byker Sunday School at the time, and were steady and well-disposed boys. George and William met in class among the Wesleyan

Methodists at the time and the latter also attended Mr. Swallow's evening school at Catterick Buildings, where he learnt to write and cypher but neither his father nor eldest brother could write. His mother relates that her sons were very affectionate and steady that after returning from their work, and when cleaned, and refreshed by their meals, they were in the habit of reading the Bible to her and never retired to rest without prayer. Many pleasing anecdotes are related by their mother, particularly of William who seems to have been her favourite son. On one occasion he said to her, 'Mother, when I'm a man I'll work hard for you, and keep you like a lady' and the mother observes that his wishes and intentions have been in a manner realized in the support she has received through the letter he wrote to her in the pit. Imagination cannot portray the scene that would take place after the breaking in of the water, and when all hope of escape was cut off. To contemplate seventy-five human beings all at once incarcerated in a living tomb, with the appalling prospect of a lingering, though certain death. They had not died from hunger, as they had killed one of the horses and had cut slices off its hind quarter, some of which were found in the caps and wallets of the men, unconsumed. They had likewise an abundant supply of spring water. The exhaustion of the atmospheric air by the influx of water bringing with it foul air, was no doubt the cause of death, probably in a day or two at the most. After the bodies were coffined, the relatives were permitted to go down the pit for the purpose of recognizing their husbands or children and Elizabeth Thew, the widow, was among the foremost. She readily recognized William's body by his fine auburn hair but what must have been her transported, yet agonized feelings, when in one of his pockets was found his tin candle-box, on which, in the darkness of the suffocating pit, or only with the dim light of his Davy lamp, the dear boy had, with a nail, engraved on his candle-box, the following touching and consolatory epistle:

'Fret not, dear mother, for we were singing while we had time, and praising God. Mother, follow God more than ever I did' and then on the other side, which, it is supposed, must have been dictated by his father, as it bears his signature, though he could not write: 'If Johnny is saved, be a good lad to God, and thy mother.
John Thew.'

Three years after the younger Johnny Thew escaped death at Heaton Main it was reported that he was killed by the rolleys at another pit.

(3) Pit: Kell

Location: Whitehaven, Cumberland
Type: Explosion
Fatalities: 20
Date: Saturday, 30 October 1819

Little is known of this disaster other than brief newspaper reports such as this from *The Times* on 5 November 1819:

On Saturday morning, a melancholy accident happened in Kell's-pit, near Whitehaven, by an explosion of firedamp, in which twenty persons were unfortunately killed. We

The image shows the extremely cramped working situations which were common in the early pits. www.cmhrc.co.uk

are informed that it was a most unexpected occurrence, every precaution having been used, and an excellent ventilation regularly preserved. The explosion proceeded from a part of the workings where the pillars are being removed, and where the atmospheric air was forced over the broken parts as much as possible. The overlookers and workmen had orders to examine daily whether any firedamp existed in this part of the pit, and on no occasion had any been perceived.

It is one of the regulations in the Whitehaven collieries, that no hewer shall approach his work without a *Davy* or *safety-lamp*; and with one he may safely explore, let the quantity of firedamp be what it may. The present lamentable event was the consequence of this regulation not being observed; and possibly the indiscretion of one individual led to the catastrophe.

These workings in Kell's-pit have been quite free from firedamp, and on Friday evening they were left in supposed safety. Impressed with the ideas of a total absence of danger, workmen become more adventurous, and are apt to consult their own convenience in the utter neglect of rules framed for general benefit. Sir H. Davy's admirable lamp, if kept in order, is perfect security to the miner. From its construction, however, the light it affords is not so strong as can be obtained by other means ; and miners are frequently induced to remove the safety-cylinder, to have recourse to candles, thereby occasioning danger, which otherwise would be avoided. Fatal as has been this accident, had it occurred an hour later more persons would probably have suffered, as a great many of the work-people of this pit had not assembled.

Two men were taken out alive on Monday morning, after having remained in the pit above thirty-six hours, exposed to the noxious vapour occasioned by the explosion, and probably owe their lives to having upon them good flannel shirts, which in a great degree preserved them from the fire, and kept them warm afterwards. These two persons, with five others, had retreated into some old workings, where the air was less impure, but their companions did not survive; and when found had no shirts upon them, and for want of covering may have perished by cold. It is surprising that the two men, a father and son, could so long exist in the place where they were, as the air was so impure that the lamps would not burn when the people went to bring them out. A little dog, the property of the two men, was also taken out alive, and was lying close by his masters.

Eighteen of the twenty victims were named as follows:

Thomas Rickerby, 22
Jacob Anderson, 24
Thomas Fraker, 24
William Askew, 28
John Cummins, 28
John Unthank, 28, left a widow and
   daughter
William McKinney
Michael Ward, 28
George Haselden, 33

James McGraa, 33
Murphy Quin, 33
Edward Cain, 37
Andrew Conroy, 37
Jonathan Castlehow, 50
Patrick Wade, 52
Stephen How, 56
Alexander McGillion, 60
Patrick McAvoy (died later from his
   injuries)

(4) Pit: Russell

Location: Wallsend, Northumberland
Type: Explosion
Fatalities: 52/53
Date: Tuesday, 23 October 1821

Wallsend was so named because it was situated not far from the eastern end of Hadrian's Wall. By the nineteenth century in the coal trade the name Wallsend had became linked to the best Newcastle coal and as such commanded the highest prices.

On Tuesday, 23 October 1821 at about 8am an explosion took place in the Bensham Seam of the colliery. The force of the blast blew a full corf up the shaft and over the pulleys which were erected above the mouth of the pit and was heard many miles away. The pit had only been re-opened for about eight weeks which meant that it was liable to be charged with gas. The workings extended no more than 100 yards in any direction. The two sections of the shaft were divided into an upcast and a downcast by timber bratticing which was entirely destroyed by the blast cutting off ventilation. Of those that were underground, Thomas Huggup, Robert Bell, Edward Coomby and William Johnson were brought out alive. Huggup and Bell were said to be uninjured but Coomby and Johnson had suffered terrible burns with Johnson succumbing to his injuries soon after. The total loss of life was given at fifty-two so, although Coomby's name was not recorded amongst the victims at the time he too must have later died from his injuries. Many of the victims had not been killed by the blast but because the brattice in the shaft was destroyed they had suffocated. John Sykes wrote an account in *Local Records*:

A dreadful explosion took place in Wallsend colliery (Russell's), by which fifty-two men lost their lives. The explosion shook the ground like an earthquake, and made the furniture dance in the surrounding houses. This alarming the neighbourhood, the friends and relatives hurried to the spot, when a heart-rending scene of distress ensued. The greatest exertions were instantly made by Mr Buddle, the viewer, who as soon as it was practicable, descended with his assistants, when a most melancholy scene presented itself. At the time of the explosion there were fifty-six men in the pit, of which number four only survived. The bodies of the deceased were most dreadfully scorched,

A sketch by Thomas H Hair showing the air-shaft at Wallsend Colliery. Author's collection

and many of them most strangely distorted. Forty-six of the bodies were buried at Wallsend, fourteen of whom, being relations, were buried in one grave; some of the remainder were buried at the Ballast hills, and some at Wallsend old church, amidst sorrowing spectators.

The owner of the colliery, William Russell, paid for the burials and presented each family with a guinea for immediate use and the promise of two shillings a week to the widows and fatherless children. They also promised that they would be housed and have fuel for as long as was needed. The majority of the victims were boys or young men. Twenty-six widows, with some being pregnant, and about ninety fatherless children were left behind.

The victims were:

William Coxon
Sam Garrett
John Richardson
James Jobling
George Roseby
John Elliott
Edward Wilson, brother to William
William Wilson, brother to Edward
Robert Bainbridge, 7
George Kyle, 11
George Thompson, 12

Michael Moon, 44, father of Michael and Alexander
Michael Moon, 12, son of Michael, brother to Alexander
Alexander Moon, son of Michael, brother to Michael
John Birtley, 12
William Bell, 45, father of William
William Bell, 16, son of William
Roger Buddle, 17
Richard Hepple, father of Richard

Richard Hepple, 17, son of Richard
John Shotton, 17, brother to Edward
Edward Shotton, 20, brother to John
Peter Hay, 19
John Gordon, 20
James Kelly, 20
William Jackson, 21
John Smith, 21
George Mason, 21
James Walker, 22
John Hutton, 22, brother to William
William Hutton, 25, brother to John
John Johnson, 23, brother to William
William Johnson, 26, brother to John
Robert Delap, 25
John Farry/Ferry, 26
Robert Bowden, 27, brother to H
    Bowden

H Bowden, brother to Robert
John Norman, 30
David Smart, 31, brother to William
William Smart, 34, brother to David
Christopher Waggot, 31, brother to
    Thomas
Thomas Waggot, 34, brother to
    Christopher
Thomas Lowrie, 32
Nicholas English, 32
Edward Campbell, 35
Thomas Davison, 36
Thomas Holt, 41
George Longstaff, 46
William Rogerson, 75
Henry Bolam, 77
George Penlington, 50, uncle to John
John Penlington, 33, nephew of George

Thomas H Hair depiction of Wallsend Colliery as it looked in 1844. Author's collection

After the explosion, John Buddle, viewer, stated:

> Accidents had always been avoided by the vigilance of two young men, the overmen of the pit. It was, however, deemed prudent in consequence of the dangerous nature of the pit, to place it under the care of the most experienced overman in the colliery. In a short time afterwards this fatal accident happened, but as the overman, together with his deputies, and nearly all the people who were in the pit at the time perished, the immediate cause of the accident could not be distinctly ascertained.

The conclusion was drawn that the overman was over confident in his judgement and had not ordered the lights to be extinguished in good time. Buddle thought that the accident had been caused by a furnace-man leaving his post to attend a feast which was being held at the time. He also was reported to have said that had there been two shafts at the pit between forty and fifty would have survived as they would have managed to get out before being suffocated.

(5) Pit: Walker

Location: Walker, Northumberland
Type: Fall of stones
Fatalities: 6
Date: Thursday, 19 June 1823

> Is a driver. Feels sick down the pit. A fortnight since was so sick the middle of the day, about 12 o'clock, that he was obliged to be carried home. Often throws his meat up in the midday. Some of them bring their meat or bait home again, not having a stomach for it. Some do not get a good feed at all, from being poor. At night shift the boys very often fall asleep and get crushed. Joseph Hobert got hurt by a stone falling on him to-day. J. H., is lame, and has evidently suffered much but he will go to work tomorrow.

An illustration depicting a boy in Walker Pit struggling to drag a loaded rolley. Author's collection

William Atkinson was cut in the head by the rollies about 8 months back, and was off 8 weeks. William Fletcher had his leg broken 8 or 9 months ago; off 5 months. His leg was nipped before. Robert Hobert had his arm broken 2 months since. Nicholas Carr had his collar bone broken.

Henry Fletcher, aged 10, Walker, 1841

Roof and stone falls were a common cause of fatal accidents in the pits such as the following which was recorded in *Richardson's Table Book*:

A most melancholy accident happened at Walker colliery, near Newcastle. An air-course having to be opened, some workmen were set to open an old shaft, which had been filled up for twenty-five years. The length of time it had been filled up, induced a belief that the earth, etc., filling it, had become united to the sides, and in consequence, the under viewer and five men unfortunately proceeded to remove the earth from the bottom of the shaft, at the same time that others were working at the top of it. They had not worked long, when the whole mass slid down, and buried them under it. Men were immediately set to work to dig them out, when they were found in a shocking mangled state all quite dead.

Four of the victims were: Thomas Copeland and William Southran, both aged 26; William Bainbridge, aged 31; and Forest Mitcheson, aged 35.

(6) Pit: William

Location: Whitehaven, Cumberland
Type: Explosion
Fatalities: 32
Date: Saturday, 18 October 1823

The William Pit was one of a group at Whitehaven owned by the Lowther family and was considered one of the most advanced mines in the country but this did not exclude it from explosions. Little is known about the disaster that took place on 18 October 1823 other than a report on 21 October in the *Carlisle Journal* which records the explosion as having taken place on a Monday but the calendar for that year shows it was a Saturday:

On Monday last, the town of Whitehaven was thrown into the utmost agitation, by an awful explosion of firedamp from the William Pit (a name of disastrous import) a coal-mine belonging to the Earl of Lonsdale, when it was known that a considerable number of colliers were at the moment employed in the workings. It was impossible to ascertain the extent of the calamity immediately, but the final certainty soon became apparent. No less than fourteen men, sixteen boys, and two girls, have come to a premature death by this catastrophe. That the pit was overcharged with firedamp in some part of the workings, is now too evident; but it is doing no more than justice to those who have the more immediate superintendence of these very extensive concerns to say, that no precaution was omitted by them to guard the colliers against any sudden accident. The workmen, it appears, were employed in removing some pillars, in a part of the pit

An early view of William Pit where thirty-two men and boys lost their lives in 1823. Author's collection

where the ventilation was extremely good, and where there was not, consequently, any reason to apprehend danger from the existence of firedamp; and indeed the air was in general supposed to be good, except in some recesses into which the colliers had no occasion to enter. They were, besides, every one furnished with a safety lamp, and were under strict orders from the superintendents to keep their lamps properly secured. When the misfortune happened, they had all nearly finished their work for the day, and by what or whose neglect or mismanagement it was occasioned scarcely a conjecture can now be formed. It is generally supposed that one of the workmen had been using some improper liberties with his lamp, and had removed the cylinder when in a place where the firedamp was present. There were also 17 horses killed, but some of their drivers escaped.

William Daniell, a landscape artist and Richard Ayton, playwright, author and sailing enthusiast, set out to travel the coast of Great Britain to record by image and written word the places they visited. One of their stops resulted in Ayton descending the William Pit. He

An artist's impression of a coalminer which was published in The Graphic. www.chmrc.co.uk

was appalled at the working conditions and the human suffering that he witnessed which was later recorded in great detail in their book *A Voyage round Great Britain,* published in 1825:

One class of sufferers in the mine moved my compassion more than any other, a number of children who attend at the doors to open them when the horses pass through, and who in this duty are compelled to linger through their lives, in silence, solitude and darkness for sixpence a day. When I first came to one of these doors, I saw it open without perceiving by what means, till, looking behind it I beheld a miserable little wretch standing without light, silent and motionless and resembling in the abjectness of its condition some reptile peculiar to the place, rather than a human creature. On speaking to it I was touched with the patience and uncomplaining meekness with which it submitted to its horrible imprisonment, and the little sense that it had of the barbarity of its unnatural parents. Few of the children thus inhumanely sacrificed were more than eight years old, and several were considerably less and had barely enough strength sufficient to perform the office that was required from them. On their first introduction into the mine the poor little victims struggle and scream with terror at the darkness, but there are found people brutal enough to force them to compliance, and after a few trials they become tame and spiritless and yield to themselves up at least without noise and resistance to any cruel slavery that it pleases their masters to impose upon them. In the winter-time they never see daylight except on a Sunday for it has been discovered that they can serve thirteen hours a day without perishing and they are pitilessly compelled to such a term of solitary confinement, with little consideration for the injury that they suffer, as is felt for the hinges and pulleys of the doors at which they attend. As soon as they rise from their beds they descend down the pit and they are not relived from their prison till, exhausted with watching and fatigue, they return to their beds again. Surely the savages who murder the children which they cannot support are merciful compared with those who devote them to a life like this.

The people in the mines are looked upon as mere machinery, of no worth or importance beyond their horse power. The strength of a man is required in excavating the workings, women can drive the horses, and children open the doors; and a child or a woman is sacrificed, where a man is not required, as a matter of economy that makes not the smallest account of human life in its calculations. In consequence of the employment of women, the most abominable profligacy prevails among the people. One should scarcely have supposed that there would be any temptations to sin in these gloomy and loathsome caverns, but they are made scenes of the most bestial debauchery. If a man and woman meet in them, and are excited by passion at the moment, they indulge it, without pausing to enquire if it be father and daughter, or brother and sister, that are polluting themselves with incest. In recording this shocking fact, I speak from authority that is not to be doubted. Great God! Can nothing be done for the redemption of these wretched slaves? It is unavoidable, that they give up almost every blessing of life; they must sacrifice soul as well as body? These dismal dungeons are certainly not fit places for women and children, the removal of whom would be an act of humanity not dearly paid for, though it should wring a few pounds from the hard economy that rules their service. The estimation in which women are held is one test of the civilisation of a people; and it is somewhat scandalous, in a country of gallant men, to see them sacrificed to the rough drudgery of coal mines. If there were nothing but the filthiness of their occupation to complain of, it would be no extravagant refinement to feel that their sex should preserve them from it; it is not a little offensive to see them changed into devils in their appearance, but it is afflicting indeed to witness the perversion that takes place in their normal character. They lose every quality that is graceful in women, and become a set of coarse, licentious wretches, scorning all kind of restraint and yielding themselves up with shameless audacity to the most detestable sensuality. Their abominations are confined during the day to the dark recess of the mines; but at night they are cast up from the pits like a pestilence to contaminate the town. We must have coals, as I have said, but we may have them through the intercession of a little humanity and liberality, without this lavish waste of morality.

Sadly it appears that there are no records of the names or ages of those that lost their lives in this disaster. There would have, in all probability, been measures taken to avoid a list being divulged to the general public as in all probability it would have included very young children and women.

(7) Pit: Croft

Location: Whitehaven, Cumberland
Type: Explosion
Fatalities: 23
Date: Saturday, 12 November 1831

Ginns and Newhouses were districts of Whitehaven almost entirely populated by miners and their families with the houses built by the Lowther family. By the twentieth century

Newhouses consisted of houses built in three long rows known as Bottom Row, Middle Row and Top Row, one behind the other on the hillside with the upper dwellings being reached by steep flights of steps. The chimneys of the lower row of houses were almost level with the bedroom windows of the upper row. The roads were extremely narrow and a single channel ran below the eaves of the front houses. There was no running water and outside sanitary conveniences were built at intervals with as many as up to six families sharing each one. Rubbish was piled up, often reaching the roof, so that waste seeped into the houses which would have been the source of disease. Although whitewashed the houses were cold, drab and unwelcoming so between their dwellings and working in the pits the families lives were harsh with pleasure consisting of gossip for the women, drinking and gambling for the men and sing-songs for all. For the male population, however, their existence was often cut short. It was more common for the little houses to be host to the mutilated body of a pit-worker from an accident who had died well before his time than to accommodate the body of a male who had passed away from old age.

At about 2.30am on Saturday, 12 November there was an explosion in the Croft Pit which was situated about a mile south-west of Whitehaven. Journalists were on the scene soon after the catastrophe and were shocked by the seemingly uncaring attitude of many of the

The image shows a few of the 266 houses built by the Lowther family for the mine workers and their families. Built on the brow of a hill, steps led from Front Row to Middle Row and Middle Row to Top Row. The last occupants of the houses were moved out in 1939 as part of a town clearance plan.
Haig Mining Museum

local people. Their story was printed in the *Whitehaven Herald* on 15 November of which these are extracts:

> Though the interest in the event, and the sympathy with the sufferers and their families was great, candour obliges us to state, that nothing seemed so extraordinary to us as comparative strangers in Whitehaven, as the very little excitement it occasioned. An event so awful in its nature, and so dreadful in its effects, would, in any but a colliery district, have excited feelings of horror and amazement, of which the effects would have been visible, in the most unequivocal manner, to the most cursory observer but though the event was indeed a subject of general conversation, it did not seem in the least to disturb the ordinary course of business, and the destruction of from twenty to thirty individuals seemed to excite less interest than in other places we have seen occasioned by the untimely death of a single human being. Even the mystery which hung over the causes of the terrible catastrophe seemed hardly to excite a desire to penetrate it and though we cannot believe that if active exertions could have been of any benefit, they would not have been spared, still, the apathy which prevailed, seemed to us a strange contrast to the deep feeling of awe and interest which elsewhere would have been occasioned by a loss of life to one tithe of the amount.
>
> About one o'clock in the afternoon we learned that the raising of the bodies of the sufferers had commenced, and we accordingly repaired to the mouth of the pit. On our road thither we saw none of those symptoms of public interest in the fate of the sufferers, which in other towns would have turned out thousands, eager to learn the least tiding of the fate of so many fellow creatures, cut off by so sudden and dreadful a calamity. The streets bore their ordinary aspects of business or of listless indifference. As we receded from the town we met successively four carts, which contained each something covered with straw, and as we learned from casual passengers, the bodies of the wretched victims. On reaching the pit we understood that five bodies had been raised, besides two living men, of whom one had since died. Fifteen or sixteen were collected at the bottom of the shaft ready to be raised, and two or three persons supposed to have perished, were yet missing and unaccounted for. About fifty or sixty persons were collected on the spot where a number of carts were ready to carry away the bodies as fast as raised, and one was pointed to us as containing the body of a young man and waiting to receive the body of his brother, who had perished along with him. Deep agony was painted in many a countenance round us and one poor young creature who had lost her husband rent the air with her wailings. The corpses were momentarily expected to be raised to the surface but we turned our steps from the scene of horrors.

The journalists attended the inquest and reported on what appears to have been a very badly conducted affair. The coroner, Peter Hodgson, the jurors and the colliery officials all had reason to be loyal to the coal-owner Lord Lonsdale. The coroner made a point towards the cause of the explosion perhaps being a miner having removed the top of his safety lamp. After going into great detail on the circumstances connected with the use of safety lamps he instructed the jury that that they must decide whether their verdict would be murder, manslaughter or accidental death. All that were involved in the inquest then proceeded to visit the houses to view the body of each of the victims. This viewing was cursory and superficial with the coroner issuing a warrant for the burials to take place the following day. The houses visited were described as 'naked, desolate and filthy' with the living

The Ladysmith Pit in the nineteenth century. Croft Pit was a few hundred feet to the north. Haig Mining Museum

occupants both male and female almost all 'either intoxicated or in a state bordering on intoxication'. On returning to the public house to continue with the proceedings those that were to give evidence were called. It was obvious that the miners who were called were hostile witnesses as one, James Floody, refused to swear an oath and became so abusive the coroner had him taken into custody but he managed to escape the arresting constable and run off. The coroner told the constable not to worry as he would report Floody so that he would never get work again. The next two witnesses were extremely drunk. Word was then brought that the bodies of William and Robert Little were ready to be examined. The younger of the two boys had no marks and appeared as if asleep. William, the elder boy, was slightly scorched and the skin of his face and chest was livid showing that he had not died quickly but had lived long enough for 'the blood to get carbonized and the skin to inflame'. They were fine looking young men who had been of good character and had almost wholly supported their aged parents. The remaining bodies were by this time all in their respective houses so the last few, bringing the total to twenty-two, were viewed and the inquest set to continue on Monday morning.

During the continuance at the police office on Lowther Street opinions were heard from Lord Lonsdale's stewards, deputies and other officials. All agreed that there had been no intimation of gas prior to the explosion and the pit was clear when it had been inspected as soon as possible after the explosion. There were heated arguments between the coroner and those not satisfied that enough evidence had been heard from the unofficial workers of the pit but the outcome was one that was to only be expected. A verdict of accidental death with no blame laid at the colliery officials' door:

> We have this week the painful duty of recording one of the most distressing accidents of a local nature that ever appeared in the columns of our paper. About three o'clock in the morning of Saturday last, an explosion of hydrogen took place in Croft Pit, to which twenty-two human beings, men and boys, have fallen victims. The cause of this heavy calamity must ever remain unknown, as no one has been permitted to survive to disclose the fatal tale. It appears, however, from the evidence given at the coroner's inquest that no blame, not even of the slightest nature, attaches to any of the viewers or deputies of the pits.

Two of the overseers, were in another part of the pit at the time the accident occurred, and one of them had just visited and examined the working where the explosion took place, and found all perfectly safe. The discharge therefore must have been sudden as well as considerable, but as the situation was a very confined one, all the men being killed within the space of two hundred yards, the effect was of course proportionally powerful. From the whole of the evidence, indeed, it is sufficiently plain that the accident was one of those inscrutable decrees of Providence, which no human prudence could either guard against or avert.

Cumberland Paquet, 15 November 1831.

Alexander Garroway had been brought from the pit alive but died on the Friday following the explosion bringing the total number of lives lost to twenty-three. Six of the victims were married and between them left seventeen children with eight of these under ten years of age:

Robert Cook, aged 19, Front Row
Hector McAllister, aged 20, Front Row
Cormick Morris, aged 60, Front Row
Abraham Taylor, aged 8, Middle Row
Arthur Queen, aged 9, son of James, Middle Row
James Queen, aged 40, father of Arthur, Middle Row
John McGaughin, aged 13, brother to Archibald, Middle Row
Archibald McGaughin, aged 23, brother to John, Middle Row
Christopher Fitzimmons, aged 14, Middle Row
John Graham, aged 17, Middle Row
Clement Ingleby, aged 20, Middle Row
Hugh Haney, aged 25, Middle Row
Thomas Wood, aged 26, Middle Row
Hugh Smith, aged 27, Middle Row

Boys employed in weighing the coal. www.chmrc.co.uk

Michael Davey, aged 26, Back Row
George Parleton, aged 42, Back Row
John McMinn, aged 17, Ginns
Patterson Turner, aged 28, Ginns
John Little, aged 20, brother to William, Gainbriggs
William Little, aged 21, brother to John, Gainbriggs
John Bolton, aged 33, Bells Lane
Robert Garroway, aged 12, brother to Alexander, Bells Lane
Alexander Garroway, aged 18, brother to Robert, Bells Lane

Peter Hodgson had told the journalists that it was in the interest of the coal-owner to prevent the occurrence of such accidents as he allowed the widows a house, coal-free for life and a pension of two shillings a week. He would also offer employment to their children 'on very favourable terms'. After this was published in the *Whitehaven Herald* these facts were disputed by a 'reputable man' who contacted the journalists. He said this was untrue, although Lord Lonsdale may give instructions to that effect they were not carried out. He told us that he knew a widow, Jane Scott, who was left with three children. She had received eight shillings a month for three years which then went down to four shillings a month for two years and then to two shillings a month for one year after which payment stopped altogether. She also only received one cartload of free coal a year. Jane made several applications to the agents but with no success. The informant added that he believed that the pensions were totally taken from the widows on the Whingill side, but that the Howgill widows had some trifle continued to them yet.

Duke Pit was on the Whingill side and William Pit was on the Howgill side.

(8) Pit: Whitley

Location: Whitley Bay, Northumberland
Type: Fall down shaft
Fatalities: 6
Date: Friday, 1 May 1835

Little is known on the early years of Whitley Colliery other than the A Pit was sunk in 1817 and the Engine Pit in 1819. This accident which claimed the lives of one man, named Robinson, and five boys sadly appears to have warranted hardly a mention. The six workers had stepped into the corf to descend the shaft at 3am to begin their shift. As the corf began to move it tilted and all were thrown out to fall a depth of about 275 feet to their deaths at the bottom of the shaft. It was found that the hook at the end of the chain had not been placed properly into the bow of the corf and had given way. The inquest found that the deaths were accidental with a deodand of one shilling was levied on the corf. (Prior to 1846 when something or someone was the immediate cause of death of a person or persons a deodand was money that was forfeited to the crown for pious uses.)

(9) Pit: Church

Location: Wallsend, Northumberland
Type: Explosion
Fatalities: 102
Date: Thursday, 18 June 1835

After the disaster of 1821 Wallsend Colliery was worked for fourteen years without major incident but in 1835 it was to be the scene of the most fatal disaster in Northumberland to date. In total about 250 persons worked at the colliery and on the afternoon of Thursday, 18 June there were 105 working below ground in the Bensham Seam of the G Pit, commonly known as the Church Pit. By the end of that terrible day 101 men and boys lost their lives and another was to die later as a direct consequence of the explosion.

The only merciful factor, if it could be described as such, was that there had been a constant stream of hewers leaving the pit from about midday until about 1.30pm, leaving putters and drivers to collect the coal and bring it to the shaft bottom, so the workforce consisted of mainly young men and boys. Only six hewers were at work. Had the explosion taken place earlier there would have been many more family men killed and subsequently more widows and children left without a means of support. It was about 2pm when a banksman had just placed an empty corve in the pit when a blast of air blew the corve out of the shaft. There was a puff of smoke and then all was still. A group of eight volunteers immediately readied themselves and descended the shaft in the hope of rescuing their comrades. Within minutes they were overcome with the noxious gas and it was with difficulty they regained the ropes to be hauled back to the surface. A large proportion of

102 men and boys perished in an explosion in 1835 at the old Wallsend Colliery. George Nairn collection

the timber brattice had fallen and closed the two shafts to the Bensham Seam. John Buddle had been viewer and underviewer at the colliery for forty-three years so would have known the workings better than anyone. He and others tried to gain access via the C Pit but everything was in ruins and tons of debris had to be brought to the surface before a search could be carried out.

As if in sympathy with the event the rain fell in torrents while women and children stood silently waiting and weeping, Davy lamps were cleaned and trimmed to give the searchers better light and group after group of volunteers descended to the chaos below. The witnesses who had been above ground told of the fire ripping through the whole of the working in less than two minutes so there would have been little hope in anyone's mind of finding survivors – but that did not deter them from trying.

It was to be the afternoon of the day following the explosion before the first bodies were found. The remains of two men and nineteen boys were brought out with some of the bodies black, shrivelled and terribly mutilated and others looking as though they were only sleeping. Miraculously, at 10pm on Saturday, three men and a boy were found alive which must have fuelled a hope in the hearts of the waiting families. The survivors were Robert Moralee, a door-keeper, aged seventy, John Brown, an onsetter, Martin Middleton, aged fourteen and John Reed, a rolley-way man. These four were found nearest to the bottom of the shaft and had probably survived because the air would have been at its clearest at that point. They had been underground at a depth of 145 fathoms since 5am on Thursday and for fifty-six of those hours they had been entombed not knowing whether the blackness that surrounded them would be the last thing they would ever see. All had suffered severe burns and two were delirious and incoherent with the effects of the afterdamp. Reed had been in the cabin and had probably been flung against the side of it as he had sustained a

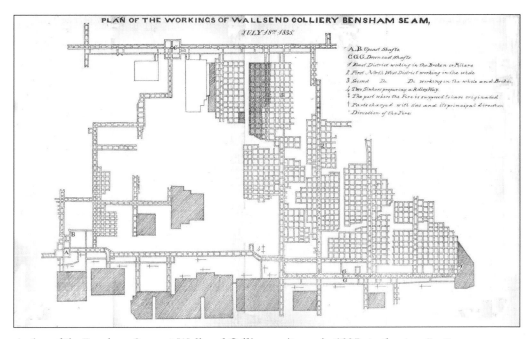

A plan of the Bensham Seam at Wallsend Colliery as it was in 1835. Author's collection

badly fractured leg. The breaks were so numerous they could not be set and on Sunday morning his leg was amputated. Not only did he have to suffer the pain of his injuries but also the grief of losing two of his sons in the explosion. It must have all been too much for his mind and body to bear as he passed away on 4 July. By Tuesday, 23 June all the bodies had been recovered except that of a young boy. His corpse was eventually found and brought to bank on 12 August. Eleven horses had also perished in the blast.

Joseph Lawson, who was born at Colliery Dyke in 1772, had been a longstanding member of the Wesleyan Society and taught at the Sunday school. He was a deputy overman at the pit so was responsible for many of the boys. Lawson's body was found about 300 yards towards the shaft from the place he had been working. Eight boys and nine young men were with him all with their lamps. Their escape route had been barred by masses of fallen timber and all had died from the effects of the afterdamp. It was concluded that Lawson had heard the initial blast and had taken the time to gather his charges and their lamps to try and lead them to safety. Those he had taught in life were with him in death.

Many of the boys that worked at the pit attended the school on Sundays and had been looking forward to a religious gala with a tea on Saturday, which had been arranged for them. Mr Reay, a teacher at the Sunday school, and his wife Dorothy, both devout members of the Wesleyan Methodist Society, had been the principal organisers and cakes and other treats had been ordered for about 400 people. A quantity of the cakes had already been made before the order could be stopped so the feast intended for the children was eaten by those left behind. Instead of the intended festivities with laughing children it would have been attended by weeping, grief stricken families.

This was Newcastle race week and a youth who was supposed to be at work that day wanted to see the Gold Cup run. Eleven-year-old James Appleby struck a bargain for the payment of a shilling to do the youth's shift when his own was ended. Young James' life was lost for the price of a shilling. A father who had lost three sons whispered to his friend that one of his sons had been so disfigured by the fire that his features were unidentifiable. He could not burden their mother with the fact that he knew it was their son only by recognising a shoe that was still on his foot. Another badly disfigured boy's body that was identified only by an item of clothing was taken to the family home to be grieved over. A short time before burial was to take place it was discovered that this was a case of mistaken identity. A body that remained unclaimed had a similar item of clothing to the boy who was about to be buried. The first body then had to be moved to the home of a family that had been frantically searching for their child for hours and the previously unclaimed body taken to his rightful place. When the four survivors were found the news a mother, who already had the body of one of her boys in her house, was brought the news that her other son had been found alive. Her joy that one of her sons had been spared was short lived as it was soon established the survivor was of another family.

A custom of the neighbourhood when a death occurred was for two young men, known as 'askers', to go into the house of the deceased. The askers would be dressed in their holiday clothes and would sit at the table which would have cheese, bread and ale upon it. Two young women dressed in mourning clothes, called 'servers' would serve the food and drink to the visitors. The askers would tell those in the house what time the burial was to take place and invite them to attend, but otherwise the entire custom would be carried out in silence. The coffin would then be brought to the door and placed on chairs and, after a hymn was sung, it would be placed in a cart. The askers would then don black scarves over their clothes and the servers would put on white hoods and precede the cart to the burial place. Over the days following the disaster this custom was repeated over and over again.

St Peter's church at Wallsend stood above the colliery workings which meant that the graves were 'set into the side of the pit'. The coffins were paid for by the mine owners who also contributed £1 for the internment of each of the following:

Robert Roseby, 8
Joseph Roseby, 10, brother to John and cousin to Joseph and Christopher
John Roseby, 15, brother to Joseph and cousin to Joseph and Christopher
Christopher Roseby, 13, brother to Joseph and cousin to Joseph and John
Joseph Roseby, 15, brother to Christopher and cousin to Joseph and John
George Kyle, 9
Joseph Wanlas, 10
Thomas Huggup, 11
James Appleby, 11, brother to Henry
Henry Appleby, 17, brother to James
John Reavley, 12
Cuthbert Reavley, 43, left a wife and seven children, father of John and Thomas
Thomas Reavley, 16, son of Cuthbert and brother to John
John Reavley, 20, son of Cuthbert and brother to Thomas
Thomas Reavley, 34, left a wife and five children, father of John
John Reavley, 11, son of Thomas
George Hall, 11, brother to John
John Hall, 18, brother to George
James Combey, 11, brother to Robert and Edward
Robert Combey, 20, brother to James and Edward
Edward Combey, 22, brother to James and Robert
Edward Combey, 12
John Hepple, 12
Bateman Dinning, 12, brother to William
William Dinning, 17, brother to Bateman
Thomas Mason, 12
Robert Mason, 13, brother to William, Peter and Luke
William Mason, 15, brother to Robert, Peter and Luke
Peter Mason, 17, brother to Robert, William and Luke
Luke Mason, 19, brother to Robert, William and Peter
John Miller, 12, brother to George
George Miller, 16, brother to John
James Miller, 20
James Moore, 12, brother to Thomas
Thomas Moore, 14, brother to James
John Robson, 35, left a wife and seven children, father of Andrew
Andrew Robson, 12, son of John
Matthew Usher, 12
Thomas Swan, 13
Christopher Raite, 13, left a widowed mother and three siblings, brother to Hutton
Hutton Raite, 18, left a widowed mother and three siblings, brother to Christopher

Robert Dawson, 13

William Thompson, 53, left a wife and eight children, father of John

James Thompson, 13

John Thompson, 14

Edward Bell, 19

Robert Bell, 13, brother to William, Richard and Francis

William Bell, 16, brother to Robert, Richard and Francis

Richard Bell, 19, brother to Robert, William and Francis

Francis Bell, 22, brother to Robert, William and Richard

John Reed, father of John and Percival (died 4 July)

John Reed, 13, son of John and brother to Percival

Percival Reed, 15, son of John and brother to John

George Soulsby, 14, brother to John

John Soulsby, 16, brother to George

Matthew Soulsby, 31, left a wife and three children

John C Waggett, 14, brother to Ralph

Ralph Waggett, 16, brother to John

John Waggott, 21, left a widowed mother and three siblings

Ralph Waggott, 75, left a wife and ten children

Francis Haxon, 14

Matthew Buddle, 14, brother to Michael and John

Michael Buddle, 17, brother to Matthew and John

John Buddle, 19, brother to Matthew and Michael

Thomas Ellerton, 14, left a widowed mother and three siblings

Luke Watson, 15

John Lowry, 15

Ralph Pendlington, 15, left a widowed mother and five siblings

David Patrick, 15, brother to William

William Patrick, 17, brother to David

Andrew Giles, 16, brother to John and Henry

John Giles, 19, brother to Andrew and Henry

Henry Giles, 21, brother to Andrew and John

James Giles, 19

Peter Green, 16

James Green, 19

George Kennedy, 16

William Crister, 56, left a wife and six children, father of William

William Crister, 17, son of William

William Wilkinson, 17, brother to Robert

Robert Wilkinson, 21, brother to William

Edward McNay, 18

Christopher Ovington, 67, left a wife and five children, father of Christopher

Christopher Ovington, 19, son of Christopher

Roger Sharp, 19

Thomas Sharp, 19, left a widowed mother

John Chicken, 19, left a widowed mother and four siblings

John English, 19

David Collins, 19, left a widowed mother and two siblings
John Stanness, 20
John Gillis, 20, left a widowed mother and three siblings
James Cousin, 20
Joseph Wright, 21
John Croser, 23, left a wife and two children
William Reay, 24, left a widowed mother and a sibling, brother to Andrew
Andrew Reay, 28, left a wife and three children, brother to William
Martin Brown, 33, left a wife and three children, brother-in-law to Robert Clark
Robert Clark, 21, brother-in-law to Martin Brown
William Johnson, 47, left a wife and two children
Thomas Simpson, 62, left a wife and twelve children
Joseph Lawson, 63, left a wife and ten children
Joseph Harbottle, 76, left a wife

There were sixty-one families affected in which there were only five surviving children capable of working. Fourteen women were left widows with forty dependant children. The amount raised by public subscription and the mine owners for the victims' families was £2009 13s 4d which was expected to last about nine years. Immediately after the disaster £2

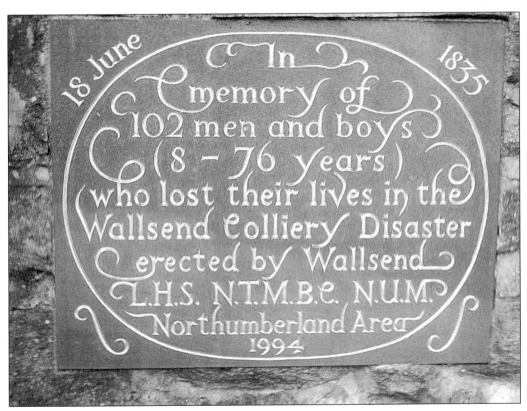

The memorial plaque dedicated in 1994 to the men and boys who perished in the disaster of 1835.
Durham Mining Museum

was given to each parent who had lost a son. The weekly allowance for a widow was 2s 6d and 1s for each child under nine years of age.

The coroner, Stephen Reed, opened the inquest at the Wesleyan chapel schoolhouse with the statement that the cause of the explosion could not possibly be ascertained. Evidence was heard with Reed giving the unusual concession of allowing some of the pitmen to ask questions of the witnesses.

The pit had been inspected by the underviewer, John Atkinson, on the morning of the explosion when he declared everything to be satisfactory. Candles were used by the hewers in the parts of the workings where it was considered safe to do so. When the pit was inspected after the accident it was concluded that the explosion had taken place in the gas-pipe drift of the Church Pit which was an area which had stood idle for many years and was known to contain firedamp. This area was sealed off by doors and if there had been any reason to enter only Davy lamps would have been used. William Thompson and William Johnson had been blasting down the roof stone to make horse-height for a new rolley-way. It was thought by the position in which Thompson's body was found that he had either opened a door leading to the pipe-drift or gas had been oozing through the door and when he came close it ignited at his candle. The fire had then travelled through the workings like a train picking up speed and exploding gas as it moved.

The verdict brought by the jury of accidental death was a foregone conclusion. Reed summed up by saying he hoped that some good would come from the deaths by serious investigations being carried out with the aim of protection in the future against this type of accident. His hopes were in vain as even the appalling fatality record of Wallsend to date did not result in any changes in legislation towards the safety of mines.

(10) Pit: Burdon Main

Location: North Shields, Northumberland
Type: Explosion
Fatalities: 11
Date: Thursday, 19 November 1835

> As to the limitation of the age of children, none should go down younger than 9. Would not actually wish for a law restricting the age of children, but yet would not entirely object to a law restricting them to 9 years of age but do not think they would be better educated for by the restriction of age. A deputation of parents would be unwilling to send the boys to schools after 9 years. Any change would be effected with difficulty among the pitmen. Even a promise to educate free of expense would not induce parents to send their children to school after 9 or 10. They would much rather see them uneducated than unemployed; thinks that after 10 they are better employed than at school. They would never make good pitmen if sent down later than 10 or 12, although there certainly are instances to the contrary. Had often had men who have been made viewers after the age of manhood but not so with drivers and putters, who must be trained to it to succeed.
>
> George Johnson, viewer of Heaton, Willington and Burdon Main, 1841

Burdon Main, also known as Collingwood Main, was situated on the north bank of the Tyne in the village of Chirton which formed the western suburb of North Shields. The latter title was used in honour of Admiral Lord Collingwood (1748–1810) who resided at Chirton and was Horatio Nelson's second in command at the Battle of Trafalgar. The pit had been worked from the seventeenth century but was abandoned for many years until taken over in 1811 by Messrs Bells, Robinson and Company. When it was reopened the skeleton of a man was found at a depth of about thirty fathoms (180 feet). There was no clue to his identity or how he met his death. The pit was considered to be 'clean' so candles were used throughout the workings. George Johnson, viewer at Heaton Colliery, in evidence to the Select Committee in 1835 recalled that on Monday, 17 July 1813 the ventilation at Burdon Main became obstructed by a creep. A group of men went below to secure timber, iron and other materials that were likely to be damaged when the gas ignited at the candles the men were carrying and caused an explosion. Eight men and boys were killed and two injured, all from North Shields. The two Richardson boys were orphaned brothers who were the sole support of their grandmother, reputed to be 102 years of age. Those who died were: Thomas Miller and William Richardson, aged 16; George Richardson and Robert Clark, aged 18; Ralph Hope, aged 24; William Hope, aged 45; Joseph Campbell, aged 46; and Ralph Wile, aged 41.

Following this disaster it was still considered that there was no need for the introduction of safety lamps, so candles continued to be used until 1835 when this decision and the habit of placing responsibility on shoulders that were far too young was to cost more lives.

It was about 3pm on Thursday, 19 November when some of the workmen in the Middle Pit heard an explosion in the adjoining workings. James Campbell, a deputy, had been doing his usual rounds when the foul air had fired his candle. The subsequent explosion was to

The old pit at Burdon Main as sketched by Thomas H Hair in 1844. Author's collection

sweep away props and devastate everything in its path. The impact of the blast and the scorching heat which followed in its wake was to take the lives of eleven men and boys. The other men were quickly got out from the rest of the workings before the afterdamp fatally affected them.

The inquest was heard at the Pineapple public house at Chirton before the coroner, Stephen Reed. When the viewer, George Johnson of Willington, was questioned he stated that he had inspected the workings about two months previously and considered the pit extremely safe. Deputy viewers went down once a fortnight and underviewers every second day. Johnson's conclusion was that the source of the explosion had been at a stopping or trap door which was looked after by a ten-year-old trapper, Joseph Arkley. He had been absent from his post and had neglected to close the door which had caused the build-up of gas. Reed decided that no further written evidence was required and stated that he felt that the trappers used were too young to be entrusted with the safety of life and property. He asked why, even if a higher rate had to be paid, the coal-owners did not employ men of middle age who would be more aware of the dangers. Johnson replied:

> It was a subject which had frequently engaged the attention of viewers and others having the management of coal-mines; that they had no means of bettering themselves. They had invariably found that boys from ten to fourteen years of age were far more tractable, attentive, and obedient than boys of a more advanced age. They had tried old men, and they found them worse than even the boys – not that they were wilfully negligent – but they lost their faculties and dozed away their time in sleep; and he did not think they could find a man of middle age who would undertake to fill such an office; there was not one about the colliery who would not think himself degraded in such a situation.

Reed answered that he thought it a pity that they did not see more clearly what was for their own good. The verdict of the jury on the following eleven victims was accidental death.

Joseph Arkley (10)
Richard Athey
James Campbell
George Clark
John Coxon
Ralph Hill
Robert Pearson
Thomas Pinkney
Samuel Robson
George Whitfield
James Wood

(11) Pit: Workington

Location: Workington, Cumberland
Type: Inundation
Fatalities: 27
Date: Friday, 28 July 1837

The children begin as trappers at about 9. We employ the trappers and drivers. The haggers employ the trailers, who begin about 12 years of age. They often trail two together when young. The corves, when full, hold coal to weigh about 4 cwt net. We have no working to dip. The trailers will have about 12 journeys to make in the day. The distance is not above 80 yards on the average, that. is from the foreheads to the staith, whence the coal is brought 300 yards by horses to the shaft. The boys assist to fill sometimes. The boys are never allowed to remain after the haggers to fill or trail. We keep an excellent air in the pit; and our working shaft is the downcast. We have had no accident with ropes breaking. The Harrington pits we work on the same system, but there we employ the trailers ourselves. There are two shafts; one is 95 fathoms deep, and the other 60. It was in the Harrington John Pit that the explosion occurred in 1838, when 24 men and 16 boys were killed, and not one was left to tell the tale how it happened; some were descending the pit at the time, and were blown out of the shaft; I should think that a fall in the air-course was the cause of it. It made sad havoc in the shaft. I was not agent at the time. Since I have had the management of that pit (since January, 1840) there has been no accident whatever – not a shilling has been paid away for accidents at all of any sort. There are 40 boys and 50 men now working in the John Pit; and in the Hodgson Pit, which adjoins it, about 30 boys and 45 men. The children very rarely work 12 hours; sometimes they do. The trappers do not work more than 10 or 11 hours on the average. We have Saint Monday, and the colliers do not work much on that day, nor on alternate Thursdays, which is the beginning of a new pay. They will work 11 or 12 hours just before pay-day. I am quite sure that the children are not ill used. In the Buddle Pit, where we do not employ the trailers, they are quite as well treated by the men as those which we employ in the Harrington pits. I should say the miners in Cumberland were as well off and have as comfortable homes as anywhere in England.

Alvan Penrice, manager of Workington Colliery, 1841

Workington Colliery had been established by the Curwen family and by 1837 the owner was Henry Curwen of Workington Hall who employed about 300 workers. Two fatal incidents had taken place at the pit in 1833, with the first an explosion on Saturday, 22 September. The Low Bottom Pit connected with the Isabella Pit but had not been worked for some time. When an attempt was made by the steward to expel a quantity of gas that had collected there was an explosion which forced the chokedamp into the Isabella Pit. Thirteen men and boys and two horses suffocated from the effects. Others were affected including John Deacon and John Hayes who possibly died as it was recorded there were fifteen killed. The fatalities could have been prevented had the steward removed the men from the pit before attempting the procedure. The thirteen that suffocated were Richard Ditchburn, John Thompson, Samuel Mulligan, ? Donald, ? Higgins, two brothers named Creen, three brothers named Brennan, and three boys: Andrew Jelly, John Watson and John

The old attempts to give hope to the young after a pit accident.
Author's collection

Hayes. Most of the victims were married with families. The second incident was in November when an inundation of water broke into the Isabella and the Lady Pits. At the time there were about thirty men and boys at work. A few managed to escape but twenty-two were trapped. Prompt action using pumps resulted in the water abating enough for a further eighteen to be rescued, leaving four still missing. The following day their bodies were found and recovered. They were George Nutter, a newlywed, aged 23; Joseph Batey, aged 24; Jonathan Weir, aged 20; and William Gallantry, aged 13. The verdict brought by the jury at the conclusion of the inquest was of accidental death. On this occasion the cost to the coal-owner was estimated at £2,000.

Until about October 1836 the manager of the colliery was Matthias Dunn who was then replaced by Ralph Coxon, a man who was either very arrogant or very stupid. He ordered that a considerable amount of the pillars should be removed, a common enough procedure, but on a large scale usually done after extremely careful planning. Making this exercise doubly dangerous was the fact that the bord and pillar area was directly under the Irish Sea. The work was continued for about two miles out under the sea on a rise which was cutting into the thickness of the covering of the sea bed between the water and the pit. The danger of the undertaking was the talk of the community and many considered it was only a matter of time before disaster would strike. Roof falls occurred, some with a considerable seepage of salt water. These early signs caused a number of the workers to leave and seek employment elsewhere. Some of those that remained, including under-agent Bowness, contacted Mr Dunn who agreed that the situation was an imminent danger and passed his fears on to a coal-owner asking him to contact Henry Curwen to draw his attention to the risk of continuing the work. If Curwen did discuss the matter with his manager then Coxon must have managed to explain his actions satisfactorily because nothing was done and the work continued. On the night of Friday, 28 July the now thin layer that had held the mighty weight of the sea collapsed and salt water poured in to the pit. The huge hole that had opened up let enough water in to fill three pits. Within an hour and a half the Isabella, the Union and the Lady Pits were completely flooded and rendered useless.

Had this taken place at any other time hundreds of lives may have been lost but it occurred just as the shifts were changing so many had already left leaving fifty-seven men

The long night waiting for news.
www.chmrc.co.uk

and boys underground. Thirty of these were about 300 yards from where the water broke in. Feeling the air current change and the pit becoming cold gave them warning that something was amiss and they immediately left by the shaft in the Bear Pit and later stated that had the trapdoors not been 'uncommonly good' they too would have perished. The twenty-seven men and boys working in the area of the inundation did not have a chance of escape and their bodies along with those of twenty-eight horses were never recovered from their watery grave. The burial service for the twenty-seven victims was conducted over the mouth of the pit. The dead were:

Martin Darling, a boy
Robert Mountjoy, a boy
Robert Mulligan, young man
John Mulligan, married, family
Hugh Cain, single
Jeremiah Murrow, single
Joseph Sharp, single
William Hayton
George McKitten, single
Thomas Ditchburn, single
Thomas Allison, married, large family
John Brough, married, large family
Jonathan Brough, widower with three children
Richard Craney, married, family
Thomas Huids, married, family
Thomas Johnstone, married, family
John Magee, married, two children
James Gambles, married, large family
Daniel Frill, married, family
John Young, large family
Phillip Dobson, three children

John Sides, married, large family
William Stubbs, large family
William Wilkinson, married, eight children
Robert Green, married, four children, son of Thomas, father of Thomas
Thomas Green, son of Robert, grandson of Thomas
Thomas Green, married, family, father of Robert, grandfather of Thomas

This appears to be one of the typical instances where the greed to win coal far outweighed the sanctity of life. Alvan Penrice took over as manager of the colliery in 1840 and when giving his evidence to the Children's Employment Commission in 1841 related the story of this disaster. He added that, had he been manager at that time, he would never have instructed that the workings be carried out to that extent. Those who died and their families were not the only ones to suffer as the flooding of the pits threw around 300 men out of work. It is also interesting to note that Ralph Coxon, the man who was, along with the coal-owner, ultimately responsible for the disaster, was not in the pit at the time. He lost his job but at least he still had his life.

(12) Pit: John

Location: Lowca, Cumberland
Type: Explosion
Fatalities: 40
Date: Wednesday, 24 October 1838

I have been three months at the pit. I trap; and get up at 4 o'clock, and get down at 5 in the morning. I do nought but open the door. I have no light. I like it very well. I have been to school; I don't go to Sunday-school. It's a good bit since I went to school; I have forgot my letters. I come out about 4, and it's sometimes rather later. I'd rather go to school than be in the pit.

John Wynn, aged 7 years 3 months, John Pit 1841

Harrington Colliery was the property of Henry Curwen of Workington Hall and employed almost 100 men and boys. It was common practice at the start of a shift for the men to wait near the shaft while the overman and his deputy entered the workings to check for foul air. On the morning of the disaster the usual procedure was followed at the John Pit with a group of men and boys standing together waiting for the instruction to head for their workplaces. This was a shift that would not commence as before the order could be given an explosion ripped through the pit with tremendous ferocity. The fire shot for many yards above the mouth of the ninety-five fathoms (540 ft) deep shaft with its force throwing debris a considerable distance. Two men and two boys had been descending in a basket which shot out of the shaft as if from a cannon. One of the men was driven over the coals at the pit mouth, a boy fell near the mouth and another boy came to rest on a ledge with his legs dangling over the edge of the shaft. The latter was disorientated but he and the man who was driven over the coals survived. The fourth man was thrown into the air and fell straight back down the shaft to his death.

A woman wrings her hands as she watches as a body is brought from the pit. Is this perhaps her husband or her son? Author's collection

In a sight that would surely haunt them for the rest of their lives the explorers found most of the victims' bodies in a charred, blackened mass fused together with corves, rolleys and other debris. The fire had torn through their midst leaving no hair on their scalps, their faces disfigured beyond recognition and their bodies mutilated. Just one young boy who was found lying beside his horse had escaped the ravages of the fire but had died from the effects of the afterdamp. The bodies of the overman and his deputy were not recovered until five days later.

An extract from the *Whitehaven Herald* on the scenes within the pit:

> The bodies of 34 of the sufferers were found nearly all together on the northern side of 'the steer,' in one frightful mass, horribly blended with corves, rolleys and various kinds of rubbish. Many of them were sadly disfigured and mutilated; their faces were blackened, the skin torn from different parts of their bodies, limbs mangled, and their hair almost invariably singed or shrivelled up into a dirty yellowish coloured matted substance. One poor boy had a stake driven through his body; in others the eyeballs were nearly forced from their sockets. These 34 unhappy beings were all, no doubt, destroyed by the agency of the fiery torrent which swept along the main workings with inconceivable fury and force. One little boy was found lying on his face beside his horse in its stable; he was not burnt or disfigured, and had died of suffocation from the chokedamp. The bodies of the overman and deputy overman were not obtained until last night; that of Key being far in the drift to the south, and Hetherington in the drift to the north.

Seventeen men, twenty-three boys under the age of eighteen and six horses had perished. For at least two of the families tragedy was already known. Jonathan and Nicholas Hayton's brother, William, was drowned in the inundation at Workington on 28 July 1837 and the Benson boys' father had also been killed at Workington. Twenty of the forty victims were under the age of sixteen with three of the boys just ten years old:

Richard Scruggam, 10
Robert Irsdale, 10
James Moore, 10, brother to William
William Moore, 12, brother to James
Ralph Sanderson, 11
George Crellan, 12
John Kelly, 12
John Ditchburn, 12
John Benson, 12, brother to Fletcher and Jonathan, left a widowed mother
Jonathan Benson, 14, brother to John and Fletcher, left a widowed mother
Fletcher Benson, 15, brother to John and Jonathan, left a widowed mother
Robert Donald, 12
? Donald, 16, cousin to Robert
John Dunn, boy, brother to Robert
Robert Dunn, 12, brother to John
Jonathan Wilson, 12, son of James
James Wilson, 35, left a wife and five children, father of Jonathan, brother to John
John Wilson, 30, left a wife and three children, brother to James
Jonathan Hayton, 12, brother to Nicholas, widowed mother
Nicholas Hayton, 14, brother to Jonathan
Henry Peel, 50, married, left one child
Robert Peel, 11, son of Henry and brother to Harrison
Harrison Peel, 13, son of Henry and brother to Robert
Eldred Burnett, 13
William Addison, 14, cousin to Thomas
Thomas Addison, 24, cousin to William
James Wynn, 16, brother to John and Robert
John Wynn, 21, brother to James and Robert
Robert Wynn, 25, brother to James and John
George Edgar, 17
John Ralph, 20
John Richardson, 22
Joseph Griminson, 22
Harrison Key, 24, left a wife and two children
Joseph Metcalfe, 25, left a wife
Henry Ward, 25, left a wife and four children
Peter Dobson, 30, left a wife and family
William Hetherington, 33, left a wife and three children
Robert Nichol, 41, left a wife and child
Joseph Cape, 52, left a wife

The inquest was held at Mr Carr's inn in Harrington before the coroner, William Bragg. The John Pit had until recently been ventilated from the Hodgson Pit but at the time of the explosion had a new air-course from the Jane Pit. It was thought that a fall in the roof had caused the new air-course to be choked up. From evidence given by the pitmen it was established that Key always carried a candle along the main passage and only used a Davy lamp to examine the actual workings. At the conclusion of all the evidence being heard the coroner appeared to lean towards the blame lying on the shoulders of the owner's agent, Lancelot Tate, in not securing the air-course but the cause related to the public by the press was that carburetted hydrogen had built up overnight in the south drift and had ignited at Key's candle. This was one of the cases where it appears rather than incur the wrath of the coal-owner someone who could not deny the charges against him was made a scapegoat.

(13) Pit: Church

Location: Wallsend, Northumberland
Type: Explosion
Fatalities: 11
Date: Wednesday, 19 December 1838

The only difference between this disaster and that of 1835 was that fewer lives were lost. The explosion took place in the same seam of the same pit, still under the command of the same viewer, John Buddle. Between 6 and 7pm eleven 'shifters' descended the pit to prepare for the following day's work by removing stones and setting up roof props. Everything was considered normal until about 9.30pm when the furnace-keeper noticed foul air at the shaft. The furnace fire was extinguished to allow explorers to descend. After several attempts to penetrate the workings they found the body of Rutherford a short distance from the shaft. He had been the last man in so it was concluded that the explosion had occurred not long after the shifters had descended. Because the explosion had not reached the shaft those on bank had not been aware that anything was amiss. After procedures were put in place to expel the foul air three more bodies were found along with that of a horse, all badly mutilated. The fiery state of the pit and the foul air meant that the bodies of the men that had been at work further in were not recovered for some hours.

Safety lamps being given out to the men at the start of their shift. www.chmrc.co.uk

The inquest was held before the coroner, Stephen Reed, at the Coach and Horses Inn at Wallsend. All that were called to give evidence stated that the ventilation was good; in fact it had been too cold for the men to strip off as they usually did when at work. No cause could be found for the explosion and the inquest was concluded with the usual verdict of accidental death on the eleven men of whom all but one were married:

Matthew Towns, single
Thomas Wilkinson, married
Hugh Row, married
William Allerton, married, two children
William Smith, married, two children
Thomas Rutherford, married, four children
Joseph Roseby, married, four children
Thomas Dinning, married, five children
John Leighton, married, five children
Jacob Maddison, married, children
Robert Bones, married, nine children

Robert Bones had kept a public house at Throckley but because of his large family was struggling to make ends meet. To earn a higher wage he had given up the public house and taken employment at the pit. He had only been at his new employment a matter of days when he was killed in the explosion.

Although hundreds of people visited the scene the journalist noted that it did not seem to cause much 'excitement' amongst those who lived in the immediate vicinity. Perhaps the loss of 102 lives three years earlier had made the community impervious towards death.

(14) Pit: William

Location: Whitehaven, Cumberland
Type: Explosion
Fatalities: 23
Date: Monday, 18 February 1839

I tried a new mode of treatment on the only man who was brought out alive, and with success. He was scarcely possessed of any vitality at all, and was in a state of asphyxia, and he had been under the treatment of brandy and emetics and hot bricks, and exposed to a pure atmosphere for three hours without effect, when I observed a bystander applying a bottle of Preston salts, containing carbonate of ammonia, to his nostrils. I immediately requested to be allowed to have the bottle, the contents of which were dissolved in warm water and administered internally. Immediately after the administration of it, vomiting was produced; and the stomach was emptied of a quantity of green vitiated fluid; he than began to rally, was placed in a warm bath for about ten minutes, was wrapped up in a pair of warm new blankets, and sent to the Earl of Lonsdale's private infirmary; where he was put to bed, and on the following morning he was able to return to his family, and might have returned to his work but that his foot had been burnt by a hot brick. He was not burnt externally, but was suffering under chokedamp, which follows the explosion of the carburetted hydrogen. Had he been burnt externally there would have been no difference: and I shall apply the same remedy next time whether they are burnt externally or not, giving two drams to each dose; repeating the dose every ten minutes. They must be treated otherwise as usual for burns. The ammonia stimulates, and is an emetic without producing lassitude and general debility as many emetics do.

Thomas Mitchell, surgeon

The second explosion of the century at this pit which was to prove fatal took place at about 2am about one and a half miles from the shaft in the direction of Parton. The only saving grace was that there were only a few men and boys on the night shift. Had it been through the day the loss of life would have been much greater. The mine had been inspected by the overman, Topping, on Saturday with no presence of firedamp being found. He had been in the act of doing a further inspection when the explosion took place. The workers had begun their shift before Topping came to their working area. He had no cause to suspect anything was amiss and was being followed by a boy carrying a lighted candle. It was later thought that there had been a sudden eruption of gas between the men leaving the pit on Saturday and returning for the Monday shift. The gas ignited at the boy's candle and caused the explosion. Because it travelled away from the overman and the boy, although both burned, they survived. An extract from *The Times* on 2 February read:

Of the 23 who perished, all, with the exception of two or three, who had evidently been burnt to death, died from suffocation, caused by afterdamp. The moment this sad occurrence was known to have taken place every means were used to restore the ventilation of the mine, in order that the scene of destruction might be approached. Some time necessarily elapsed before this could be accomplished, and several of the stewards and others engaged in this dangerous employment were frequently brought to the pit-mouth, from the unwholesome state of the atmosphere below, in a state of complete exhaustion. At 6 o'clock yesterday evening the last body was discovered and brought up; it was that of a boy named Joseph Clark.

A list of victims (one name not known) is as follows:

Joseph Clark, a boy
Robert Tear, 12, brother to James, Addison Alley
James Tear, 18, brother to Robert, Addison Alley

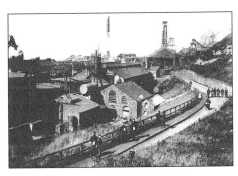

The miners, carrying their water bottles, walk along the road to begin their shift at the William Pit. Haig Mining Museum

John Ross, 18, Charles Street
John Firth, 33, married, two children, Charles Street
Barney Cairn, Tangier Street
Felix McGinnis, 33, married, two children, Tangier Street
Thomas Gilmore, 60, married, three children, Tangier Street
Hugh Raney, 46, married, four children, Banks Lane
The following victims resided at Newhouses:
John Fisher, 10
William McMullen, 11
John Dunn, 11
Michael Wheatley, 13
William Doran, 14
Christopher Pearson, 14
William Atkinson, 14
Richardson Shields, 16
William Smith, 22, newly married
John Tordiff, 31, left a pregnant wife and four children
William Davidson, 41, married, four children
Richard Harrison, 43, married, four children
George Scott, 60, married

In February 1829, the *Carlisle Journal* printed this observation:

The accident is one of those awful circumstances which spread misery and distress throughout the whole of the neighbourhood and leaves many a house in wretchedness by depriving them of protection and support. It is also one of those occurrences against which no human foresight or precaution could have effectually protected those who became its victims.

(15) Pit: Bigge

Location: Willington, Northumberland
Type: Explosion
Fatalities: 32
Date: Monday, 19 April 1841

Looks about 7. Keeps a door; has been down the pit half a year; gets up at 3 o'clock a.m. and goes to work at 4 o'clock. Works at the Low Pit. John Black and other rolley drivers beat him sometimes with their hands. His door is close at the shaft. Is not frightened. Gets upon his uncle's (the overman) knees, and goes down with him. Cannot read at all, or write. Goes to the (Methodist) Sunday-school. Goes to no other school. Goes to chapel every Sunday.
Thomas Dotchin, aged 6, Willington Colliery 1841

Has been down the pit 1 year. Keeps a door. Get up at 3 o'clock a.m. Goes down the pit at 4 o'clock; comes up at 4 o'clock and sometimes later; does not know how often but it is very often. Is sometimes beaten a little by drivers, by their hands, and with their whips a little; not much to hurt. Does not go far in by (about 300 yards). Goes down by riding upon the knees of anybody in the loops, the men, or big putters. Cannot read at all; does not know his letters; has been only to a Sunday-school; does not go now. His brother is a hewer. Has two brothers down the pit, Jack puts, and Bill drives.

James Strong, aged 7, Willington Colliery 1841

In *Local Records* John Sykes recorded that in December 1829 four men lost their lives due to an explosion followed by an inrush of water and in March 1840 three men and five boys were severely burnt, one of whom died the following day. Thomas Hair recorded that an attempt to sink a staple from the Wallsend to the Bensham Seam in September 1831 had resulted in an explosion which had instantly killed three men and eight horses. Fourteen men were terribly burnt and four subsequently died of their injuries. The Bensham Seam of the Bigge Pit was then abandoned because of the presence of a large blower of gas but by 1841 it was decided by the owners, Matthew Bell, Dixon Brown and George Johnson, to reopen the seam. The area of excavation was still very limited when, at about 1.15pm on 19 April, there was a rush of wind and dust from the shaft. Those on the surface knew this was the sign of an underground explosion.

When explorers descended the 840 feet to the seam they found the workings of the mine were covered in a thick layer of dust and the stables were alight. One person was still alive but he died before reaching the surface. Two men, Michael Ranson and Henry Dunn, and a boy, George Charlton, who were working on the eastern side of the shaft and well away from the seat of the explosion escaped unhurt. James Pearson, Robert Black and John Crawford were alive when they were brought to bank but their injuries were so terrible that their deaths later that evening would have been a merciful end to their suffering. A total of thirty-two men and boys along with two horses perished. Twenty-six hours after the disaster

Willington Colliery as sketched in 1844 by Thomas H Hair. In 1841 an explosion claimed thirty-two lives in the Bigge Pit at this colliery. Author's collection

a pony was found starving and thirsty but alive. This pony was lame and blind and was a special favourite having been in the mine longer than even the oldest workman could remember and its survival was considered a miracle.

The inquest was held at the Engine public house before the coroner, Stephen Reed. George Johnson, senior viewer and part owner of the colliery was also present. As evidence was heard it was established that gas had fired at the candle of George Campbell who was the son of one of the deputies, Thomas Campbell, but, where did the gas come from?

The cause was given as a trap-door being left open by nine-year-old Richard Cooper causing an accumulation of gas had built up and then igniting at the candle of the putter, Campbell. Robert Williamson, a hewer, gave evidence stating that Cooper had never neglected his door and was steady and reliable. His evidence was discounted by Reed who decided that the dead boy was the cause of the explosion even though there was no proof to support this theory. The jury acted on Reed's direction and returned a verdict of accidental death. This was the second time during an inquest held before Reed and where George Johnson was present that a young dead boy had been blamed as the cause of multiple deaths.

Although still unsubstantiated, a later statistical report to the Select Commission stated that Richard Cooper had been found some distance from his post and that the explosion could not have blown his body that far. It was said that he had gone to play with two other boys, leaving his door unattended, perhaps propped open, and this story was held as fact. Others who had knowledge of pit accidents thought that the neglect of a door could not have produced such results and that the explosion had been caused by a sudden outburst of firedamp.

Many of the following thirty-two victims were buried at St Bartholomew's, Longbenton:

Thomas Bolton, 9
Richard Cooper, 9
George Scott, 9
Robert Pearson, 9, brother to Thomas
Thomas Pearson, 15, brother to Robert
James Pearson, 18
Simpson Mason, 10
William Martin, 10, son of Michael
George Martin, 19
Robert Brown, 19
William Bainbridge, 11, brother to Thomas
Thomas Bainbridge, 18, brother to William
John Brown, 13
Robert Campbell, 14
George Campbell, 18, nephew of John
John Campbell, 34, uncle of George
James Liddell, 14
Matthew Ranson, 15
Robert Black, 15
John Hall, 16
Joseph Crosby, 17
Jonathan Crosier, 20
John Crawford, 22

John Joyce/Jowsey, 23
William Howey, 24, married, two children
William Dodgson, 25, brother to Thomas
Thomas Dodgson, 27, married, brother to William
Joseph Johnson, 27
John Reed, 28
Michael Martin, 36, married, four children
William Coxon, 36, married, child
Thomas Wood, 39, married, six children

The following is an extract from evidence relating to the disaster given to the Children's Employment Commission by John Johnson who had been acting in the absence of the chief viewer of Willington:

I was at home when the explosion happened, and in twenty minutes was at the Bigge Pit and saw the only people who escaped unhurt. These were two men and a boy who had been at work making a rolley way, 500 yards east of the pit. They were made aware of the explosion by the sudden rush of wind and dust past them. On examining the men, they said they ran out immediately on hearing the noise, in the dark, their lights being extinguished; on arriving at the bottom of the pit, which they had some difficulty in doing, owing to several falls one from the roof of the mine, in consequence of the timber being blown out, they found the cage fast, it having been damaged by the explosion; they disengaged it and ascended by the other cage that was sent down to them. I immediately descended, accompanied by the under viewer and several workmen, who cheerfully volunteered to render every assistance at this dangerous time, each man having his Davy lamp. It was some minutes before our eyes became accustomed to the horrible gloom, although groans were heard from some of the poor sufferers; at the bottom of the shaft we found two lads, one an onsetter, the other a rolley-driver, both of them alive; they were sent to bank but survived a very short time. Lying near to them two other lads quite dead, all these poor fellows were dreadfully burnt. My first object to examine the way to the west but we had not proceeded more than six or seven yards we came to an immense fall of the roof, occasioned by the timber that supported it having been blown away. Near these falls were lying a horse and pony, severely burnt and mangled, they were quite dead. We continued west for forty yards where we met with the afterdamp, but hearing a groan up the north headway, we rushed up for fifty-six yards and succeeded in bring out a body but being much burnt he could not be known. He died after being taken to bank, where he was recognised as James Pearson, a putter. Having persevered for this distance without air and in the afterdamp, we had great difficulty turning, feeling quite sick and giddy. In our way up the headway we found that the stoppings were blown out and that consequently the current of air had ceased to ventilate the entire west and north workings and that all the people who were in that part the pit, who might have escaped the effects of the explosion, would lose their lives by the afterdamp.

Although the evidence appeared conclusive there were some who did not believe that the neglect of the door in question could have led to such fatal results and that the explosion was more than likely to have been due to a sudden outburst of firedamp.

Part Three

Fire, Air and Water

1844–1888

The Angel of Death spread his wings on the blast,
And breathed in the face of the foe as he passed;
And the eyes of the sleepers waxed deadly and chill,
And their breasts but once heaved, and forever grew still.

(16) Pit: Duke

Location: Whitehaven, Cumberland
Type: Explosion
Fatalities: 11
Date: Thursday, 11 January 1844

The Duke Pit had been inspected at about 10am on Thursday by the overman, John Armstrong, who found the working areas to be in a good state. Although safety lamps were in use it was considered safe to remove the tops, which of course rendered the 'safety' element of the lamps useless. Fifteen men and a boy descended the shaft at 3pm to begin their shift and at 5pm a loud blast was heard giving the indication to those on the bank that the pit had fired. Armstrong, Benjamin Cowan, John Fitzsimmons and Edward Welch descended the shaft to find three men and a boy at the bottom all alive but suffering from the effects of chokedamp. After getting them in the basket and sending them to bank they continued inbye to find three dead horses about sixty yards from the shaft and another seven that had perished in the stables. About 200 yards past that point they came upon the first body and then the body of Benjamin Cowan's son. Continuing the search, the bodies of another nine men were found straggled out over a distance, as if they had warning of the danger and had tried to escape.

The inquest into the cause of death of the eleven victims was held before Mr Lumb, coroner, at the Public Office. After viewing the bodies and hearing from witnesses he summed up by saying:

The evidence, which had been laid before them, had been given in so clear and straightforward a manner he did not think the jury would have much difficulty in coming to a conclusion. He remarked that it appeared from the evidence of several witnesses it was a common practice for the men to work with the tops of their Davy

Bodies being removed from a pit with coffins lying at the ready. Author's collection

lamps off, and that there was no doubt, had they been on, the accident would have been prevented. The only question for consideration was whether the death of the men whose bodies they had viewed was accidental, or might have been prevented by the use of any responsible precautions. It was gratifying to think that the surgeons had displayed so much promptitude and courage in going down the pit, after the accident, to render assistance. In conclusion he had no doubt that the verdict of the jury would be satisfactory to the manager of the pit, to the men engaged in it, and to the public at large.

The jury returned a verdict of accidental death on the eleven victims, listed below:

William Robinson, 19, son of William
William Robinson, 47, married, seven children, father of William
Launcelot Atcheson, 20, brother to John
John Atcheson, 22, brother to Launcelot
Benjamin Cowan, 21, married
Thomas Salaney, 22, married, child
Peter Pladdy, 23, married, child
Joseph Brown, 26, married, three children
Bernard McAmarty Hughes, 27, married, child
John McCashem, 27, married, two children
George Clockson, 23

These lines were written on the evening of the disaster:

O God most mighty! Most supreme! Most high!
By whom we live, at whose decree we die
Inspire my soul! assist me to explain
Those mis'ries, which, a mortal fails to name

Help me to lay, before a gen'rous world
The sudden woe, in which the widow's hurl'd
Show me how much, a host of infants claim
The help of those who bear the Christian name.

The wind is whistling now, o'er many ahead
That's weeping sadly for a husband dead
And many a prattling child, with anguish sigh
To know the cause, for which their mothers cry.
Alas! poor infant, little dost thou know
The cause, which fills thy parent's heart with woe
That he, who but an hour, or two before
Was thy fond father – but is now no more!
Has ceased to smile upon thy speaking face
Has ceased, to run the all-important race.

Methinks I hear the carts go rumbling on
Containing this, – a father, that-his son
And now I see a youth, before the fire
Outstretched lies beside his frigid sire
While all the latent ties of flesh and blood
Breathe sighs to nature, and Heave groans to God
Another cart! how murmuring the sound
Which passes slowly o'er the ill paved ground
Containing – Who? the impatient kindred cry
'Brothers! Two brothers!' is the sad reply.

(17) Pit: Dearham

Location: Maryport, Cumberland
Type: Shaft Accident
Fatalities: 5
Date: Saturday, 24 August 1844

The colliery was owned by Messrs Ostle and Dunglinson and was situated near Maryport. The accident that took place in August 1844 was described in the press as a 'dreadful miscalculation'. As the basket was being lowered down the shaft, just a few feet from the top, the rope broke sending the five occupants hurtling to the bottom, a depth of about 150 feet. Two were brought up alive but breathed their last within a few minutes. An inquest was held the same evening where accusations that the rope had been deliberately cut were looked into. The rope was comparatively new and was supposed to bear a weight up to 60cwt. The basket and the persons in it would have been no more than 5cwt. After much deliberation the jury found that the accusations were no more than rumours and that the rope had been defective so the deaths were accidental.

One boy had a lucky escape. He had attempted to get into the basket but had not felt safe as he felt there were too many persons so had turned back to wait for the next descent.

On the Sunday a large amount of people attended the burial of the victims at St Mungo's church in Dearham:

Wilfred Lister, 8, brother to Benjamin
Benjamin Lister, 12, brother to Wilfred
William Callthorpe, 17, brother-in-law to Thomas Ostle
Thomas Ostle, 24, married, three children, brother-in-law to William Callthorpe
William Murray, 39, married, five children

(18) Pit: West Moor

Location: Killingworth, Northumberland
Type: Explosion
Fatalities: 10
Date: Thursday, 3 April 1845

By the 1840s Killingworth Colliery was owned by Lord Ravensworth and was recorded as employing 200 to 300 men. On Thursday, 18 January 1844 there was what was described as a 'slight explosion' at the West Moor Pit in which six men were severely burnt. Five of the victims later died of their injuries. It was thought that a fall of stone had caused gas to escape which had ignited at one of the men's candles. The verdict was 'accidental'. Those who were burnt were Thomas Bates, William Richardson, Joseph Hindmarsh, William Hardy, John Nicholson (aged 37) and John Storey (36). The latter three were married with families.

On the night of 3 April 1845, at the same pit, an explosion was to claim a further ten lives. Had this occurred during the day there would have been many more victims. The first indication of disaster came from two hewers. They described the explosion as 'coming back on them' from the workings. The air in the workings rushed along the drift to the pit mouth, carrying with it dust particles which gave the indication at the surface that there had been an underground explosion. A continuous stream of water was directed down the shaft and this helped the rescuers.

At the inquest a collier said that the pit was safe an hour before the disaster. Joseph Browner, overman, stated that he had inspected the pit and found it safe. John Wales,

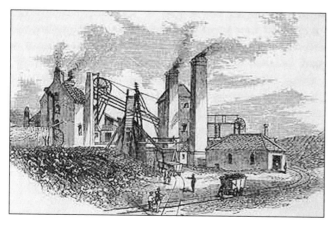

Killingworth Colliery as sketched by Thomas H Hair in 1844. Author's collection

Another view of Killingworth Colliery sketched in 1844 by Thomas H Hair. Author's collection

viewer, said that lamps were not needed in the pit. The cause of the explosion was thought to be from the discharge of a large quantity of gas from a fault that had been pricked two or three weeks previously. A group of men had descended the pit carrying safety lamps but John Hindmarch, a young boy, had preceded them carrying a candle. It was thought that a blower had ignited at his candle and this was the cause of the ignition.

The inquest, heard before the coroner, Stephen Reed, was held on the day following the explosion and appears to have been a farce. It was reported in the *Gateshead Observer* that the first day's evidence was taken from a copy of the *Newcastle Journal* and not the coroner's own notes. It was further reported that one of the jurymen had failed to appear, so Reed made a replacement with his own coachman who attended in his livery. The coroner informed the journalists that they were there 'under sufferance' and were to write only his own words and nothing else. By this time, however, not all the newspapers were subservient to the coal-owners and Reed was criticised strongly in the *Advertiser* both for his handling of the journalists and his haste in providing a substitute juror. Reed wrote to the *Newcastle Journal* with his explanation which was that he had other business to attend to and if he had delayed the inquest the bodies would have been in the homes of their families until the following Tuesday. He claimed that his coachman was intelligent, could read and write and was impartial, all the attributes a juryman required.

The summarization at the conclusion of the inquest was that there was no fault with the ventilation of the colliery and a verdict of accidental death was returned on the ten victims who were all buried at St Bartholomew's at Longbenton:

William Moulter, 11
Thomas Stewart, 11
John Hindmarch, 'young boy'
John Gray, 19
Matthew Thomson, 21
Thomas Thompson, 32, married, five children
Robert Hall, 24
John Sharp, 40, married, six children, brother to William
William Sharp, married, seven children, brother to John
Peter Tweedie

In September 1845, the potato blight began to affect the crops in Ireland. Over the next few years thousands of families left their homeland to avoid starvation which produced an influx of workers being employed in the coalmines. In the succeeding years disaster lists began to include many more Irish names than previously.

(19) Pit: Whinney Hill

Location: Cleator Moor, Cumberland
Type: Explosion
Fatalities: 30/31
Date: Saturday, 28 October 1848

The town of Cleator Moor developed principally with the influx of Irish immigrants seeking employment in the ironworks of which building began in 1842. The Whinney Hill and Hope Pits were leased by the Hermatite Mining Company in the 1840s and supplied coal for the furnaces of the ironworks to make high grade steel. Whinney had different spellings such as Whinny, Wynie and Whinnie. There appears to be little information on this pit until the disaster which took place about 6.30 on a Saturday morning in October 1848. There are conflicting reports on the number of those in the pit and the survivors. Most state that at the time of the explosion there were thirty-one men and boys at work of which only one survived, but the list compiled of those killed numbers thirty-one and there is mention of two survivors. One of those who escaped death would have been the furnace-man who was stationed in the shaft and would have been able to reach the pit bank comparatively quickly. Edward Bradley did not make his escape so easily and, in fact, his survival was seen as something of a miracle. Young John Ward was brought out alive but died soon after from severe burns to his face. The following is the list of those recorded as fatalities:

Henry Mash, 12
Robert Clark, 13
John Ward, 13
Richard Lawson, 12, son of Richard and brother to John
John Lawson, 16, son of Richard and brother to Richard
Richard Lawson, 46, married, seven children, father of Richard and John
John Aiken, 17, son of Thomas
Thomas Aiken, 39, married, five children, father of John
James Dowie, 18
John McLaughlin, 18
John Milby, 18, brother to James
James Milby, 26, brother to John
George Watson, 19
Charles Lochery, 21
Daniel Lochery, 32, married, child
John Disley, 22
Alexander Davidson, 23, married, child
William Lish, 23, married, two children
William Dryden, 23

John Cummins, 24, married, two children
Thomas Fitzsimmons, 25, married
Dennis Savage, 26, married, family
James Thompson, 26, married, four children
John Barwise, 28, married, two children
James Harrison, 29
John Hall, 30, married, three children
Patrick Kelley, 31, married
John Atkinson, 32, married, two children
Patrick Monaghan, 41, married, seven children
John MacDouall, 46, married, child
George Veitch, 47, married, nine children

Unbelievably, the matter of the inquest to be held on how the victims met their deaths became an object of dispute. The pit was within the district of which Mr Bragg was coroner but some of the victims had resided in the district of which the coroner was William Lumb. According to the *The Times* this was resolved by both coroners holding separate inquests:

> The consequence of this has been an unusual degree of activity on the part of each functionary, both of whom, however, have persevered in their assumed right with every regard to public decency; and whilst giving considerable employment to medical men, parish constables, and jurors, by the frequency, length, and strictness of their investigations, have each manifested a disposition to bring to light any circumstances tending to establish or disprove the rumoured foulness and bad ventilation of the pit in question.

A Victorian sketch depicts the panic as the sound of an explosion brings the mining community rushing to the pit mouth. Author's collection

Statements were given by officials who were responsible for the inspections of the pit. Some of the workers at the pit were also questioned including the survivor, Edward Bradley. His testimony was extracted with some difficulty as being a Roman Catholic he initially refused to swear on the Testament as it was not his bible and he considered that swearing on it did not bind him to speaking the truth. Eventually he was persuaded and was sworn. He is reported as saying:

I am a hagger [hewer] at the Whinny-hill pit. I went to work there on Saturday morning at half-past 4 o'clock. My fellow partner was John Cummins. We went down to work in the Bannock-band. We got up to our place of working, where we were sitting when John Atkinson's underman, Daniel Lochery, came and had some words with Cummins, and said he would knock his brains out with a hammer. In a quarter of an hour afterwards Cummins left me, and I never saw him again alive. I heard an explosion between 6 and 7 o'clock. I was lifted off my feet, and then made my way to the shaft, 300 yards off. As I proceeded along I found the chokedamp getting stronger. I saw plenty of dead men about. I got up by the rope, and into the basket, which was empty. I shouted as hard as I could to the banksman, and was taken up immediately. I was weak and stupefied when I got to the top. I walked home in about two hours. We work with Davy lamps. I have worked with the tops off. We never went without the work being examined before us, by the master or shiftsman. We have been ordered by the shiftsman to be careful. I examined the working myself, I think the pit was fired within 20 or 30 yards of the shaft by a naked light, but I do not know by whom. There is no candle used in the pit. There were no horses in the pit.

He was then asked how they managed without horses, and replied:

We make horses of ourselves; if the horse can't do the work a man is forced to do it. The pit is sometimes dirtier than other pits. The ventilation is sometimes good and sometimes bad; it is often so. I never made a complaint of the pit being foul and dirty. I came out when the air was too foul. When I went down into the pit that morning the air was as usual, but as I passed the place where I think the explosion was it was something adulterated – it was middling. I lost my lamp where I believe the explosion was. I was trampling over dead bodies. The upper end of the pit was in a good state of ventilation.

The results were inconclusive although it was suggested that a man, probably Cummins, had removed the top of his safety lamp to light his pipe. Gas had then ignited at either the naked light or the pipe. It is certain that the pit was in an extremely dangerous state but the jury brought a verdict of accidental death with the coroner pointing out that if a person smoked in a coal-pit and caused death by this action he could be charged with wilful murder. He advised if caught in the common and dangerous act of smoking the person should be brought before the justices and punished.

Cleator Moor was to be the scene of a further tragedy when on 25 May 1863 work was taking place to connect Number Two Pit with the Hope Pit which was about 700 yards distant. Brothers John, William and Alexander Weir and Alexander's ten-year-old son were all overcome by noxious gas and suffocated. Between them the three brothers left behind wives and fourteen children. The inquest concluded with a verdict of accidental death with a recommendation that the coal-owners employ more efficient overmen so that colliery rules were more strictly adhered to.

The recommendations appear to have fallen on deaf ears as another explosion took place at the pit on 14 July 1850. Perhaps because this was a Sunday and the pit was not fully manned, there was no loss of life but the workings suffered considerable damage. The shaft was badly damaged by fire and it was recorded that it had been known for some time that the pit was in a dangerous state.

(20) Pit: West Moor

Location: Killingworth, Northumberland
Type: Explosion
Fatalities: 9
Date: Friday, 31 October 1851

On 31 October 1851, another nine lives were to be lost at West Moor Pit due to an explosion. The cause remained a mystery but it was suggested that, contrary to orders, a man had taken gunpowder and candles into the workings. Just over a week before, William Simpson, a hewer had been working in the same district using a candle. There had been a small explosion in which he was badly burned. He died from his injuries the day before this disaster. When the area that Simpson had been working in was examined by a management party they found nothing to account for the explosion.

The *Newcastle Chronicle* described the inquest on the deaths of 31 October as follows:

> A number of pitmen called as witnesses by Mr Brewis, the solicitor who appeared for the Miners' Association, failed to incriminate the masters or show that the pit had been neglected. Some of the men said they had been afraid to work at the pit, yet they had continued to work at it until the time of the explosion, and would have continued doing so had it not taken place. They had never complained to the viewer or his underviewers concerning it. No complaints had ever been forwarded to the Government inspector either, and that gentleman did not see the pit until after the explosion. There was a considerable difference of opinion between the pitmen and viewers that were examined regarding the comparative merits of the Stephenson and Davy lamps. The Stephenson or 'Geordy' lamp was preferred by the men; the Davy by the viewers. The peculiar characteristic of Stephenson's lamp is that it extinguishes itself upon the presence of gas; the gauze of the Davy turns red hot. Either of those indications is a warning to the men to leave the pit, which, upon their own evidence, they had not done in every instance. The opinion of Mr Dunn, the government inspector, was that a violent discharge of gas had suddenly taken place either from the top coal or from a fissure in the coal. The back cast drift seemed in his opinion to have been the scene of the greatest violence, and a slight derangement of the brattice, especially if the furnace were slackened, might cause an accumulation of gas. He thought there was sufficient air sent into the district for all the ordinary working purposes of the pit, but the margin between safety and danger being so slight he recommended that an additional quantity of air be sent into those workings to meet a contingency similar to the one that had now happened. The immediate cause of the explosion was a mystery to him as to the other

viewers. A Davy lamp had been known to fire where there was a brisk current of air, but in this district the air was sluggish. The coroner, after the inspector gave his evidence, summed up, and the jury returned a verdict of accidental death.

Stephen Reed had headed the inquest on William Simpson and on the subsequent nine victims. He stated that in his experience the owners generally spared no expense to prevent accidents and they were usually caused by the men themselves. During the investigation it became evident that the ventilation had been very much decreased due to the extreme wetness of the upcast shaft. Repairs were completed after the accident and the ventilation was much improved but these measures were too late for the victims and their families. Some of the victims were buried in St Bartholomew's churchyard at Longbenton. The name of one boy remains unknown:

Robert Gordon, 'boy'
William Mason, 12
George Campbell, married, two children
Robert Carr, married, three children
William Hay, married, two children
Jacob Hedley, married, three children
George Gray, married
William Hewitt, married

(21) Pit: Greenlaw Walls

Location: Berwick-on-Tweed, Northumberland
Type: Inundation
Fatalities: 5
Date: Wednesday, 8 April 1857

The new Greenlaw Walls Colliery was near Duddo, about ten miles south of Berwick and was owned by Mrs Johnson and Messrs Carr. The pit had two workable seams, one at ten fathoms (60ft) which was three feet thick and one at eighteen fathoms (108ft) deeper which was two and half feet thick. The latter seam was being worked at the time of the disaster. The workings in both seams were described by Matthias Dunn at the time as 'very ancient' and there were no plans of the old neighbouring pits, only traces of them and the knowledge of the old colliers which was taken into account when the pit was sunk. The new pit had a bratticed shaft, nine feet in diameter with an engine on both sides that pumped water and raised coal. The upper coal seam was found to have been worked and was drained, the coal in the lower seam appeared not to have been touched. When the drifts were started, water, tinged with red, came from the coal which was a warning that it was from an old waste. When the drifts reached sixty yards, the men urged the overman, Thomas Ray, to start boring in the headings. This request was passed on to the resident viewer, Mr. Bayles and although he had been in the workings the day before the disaster, he decided that boring was not required. As the work was being carried out the south drift suddenly holed into a drowned waste. The seam was thin and the workings narrow and it was soon filled with water killing all the people in the pit. There was a delay in three men at the surface being

A Victorian illustration of the burial of a miner.
www.cmhrc.co.uk

able to descend and attempt a rescue as they had to wait for the banksman who was having his dinner at the time. The five victims were: Thomas Patterson, John Robson, Andrew Oliver and two young men named Hogarth. Between them the victims left four widows and ten children.

Although the jury of twenty men at the inquest concluded that the accident was due to Bayles and his superiors placing the pit so close to old workings and disregarding the request of the men to bore, a verdict of accidental death was returned.

(22) Pit: Burradon

Location: Burradon, Northumberland
Type: Explosion
Fatalities: 76
Date: Friday, 2 March 1860

Until the sinking of the first pit at Burradon in 1820 the vicinity had been sparsely populated with the area mainly agricultural and a small freestone quarry employing just a few men. From towards the end of the 1820s, small houses were built by the coal-owners in close proximity to the pit to house their workforce and gradually the population increased.

Burradon and the nearby Seghill Colliery had both been owned wholly by the Carr family but were sold in July 1858 to different owners which required the pits to be separated. Joshua Bower was the owner of Burradon with the Carr family still holding shares. Charles Carr stayed on as viewer, a post he had held since 1849, and also retained a financial interest in the mine. The two pits were joined by an interconnecting door which Matthias Dunn,

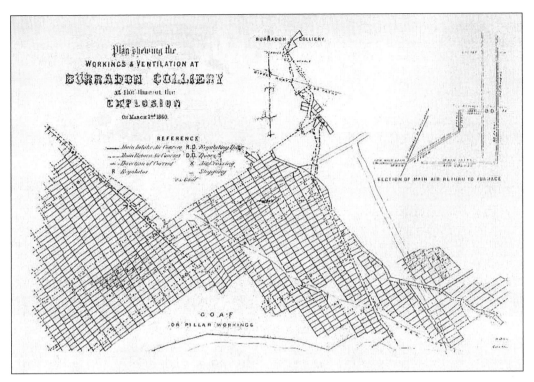

A plan of Burradon Colliery at the time of the explosion of 1860. Author's collection

Inspector of Mines, recommended should be blocked off upon the sale. The Burradon shaft, which was at a depth of 180 feet, became the upcast shaft with the stone work around it raised to protect it from the west winds and a furnace built halfway down. This heated the air causing it to rise and draw air through the workings from the downcast shaft. Because greater production was now expected from the colliery due to the huge demand for coal a larger winding engine was installed and changes were made so that the shaft could draw four tubs instead of the previous two. These alterations meant there had to be changes to the system of ventilation. Both Davy lamps and, in some parts of the workings, candles were used.

On 24 December 1858, the miners wrote to Dunn asking him to inspect the colliery as the men thought it in an unfit state to work in. The pit was duly inspected and found to be satisfactory although there were areas where there were obstructions in the ventilation due to the waste. Dunn also detected gas in a goaf so made some recommendations for improvements. Towards the end of 1859 some of the miners again became concerned about the amount of gas that had become present in the pit. John Carr, William Dryden and George Maddox were the most vocal in their opinion to those in charge and on one occasion the workforce was evacuated by the deputies but this had been considered to be a false alarm and further complaints were virtually ignored. On the day of the disaster John Carr had told his wife he was so worried about the state of the pit that he was not going down. His wife asked how they were going to live if he did not go to work so, with misgivings, he donned his clothes and left the house. This was to be the last time his wife was to see him alive. On 30 January 1860 Dryden noticed his candle was burning with a large blue flame which was a sure indication of the presence of gas so he left the pit before his shift was over. When he reached the bank he told the overlooker that he was not willing to go back down because of his fears that something was about to happen. Dryden was dismissed which ultimately was to save his life. At 1am on Friday, 2 March, Walter Nicholson, fore-overman, descended the pit and carried out the normal procedure as to an inspection of the workings. At 9am, declaring everything to be satisfactory, he left the pit with 111 men and boys already at work or about to commence their shift.

Thomas Maddox, George Allen and his brother Robert were working in a gaseous part of the mine when, at about 1.30 that afternoon, there was a blast of air accompanied by small pieces of flying coal. The horses became distressed and although the men knew this had not been a large explosion it was enough to make them decide to leave. In other parts of the workings the men noticed the air current change direction and they too decided to evacuate the pit. As they headed for the shaft they met the back-overman, William Alderson, who was heading inbye with a group of workers. Alderson tried to get the men to return to work but they refused. Most of those trying to escape the pit had reached the lamp cabin, which was about 500 yards from the bottom of the shaft, when there was a tremendous explosion. The Davy lamps were extinguished and men, boys and horses were knocked off their feet as debris whirled around them. After helping those around them get to the shaft and safety the Allen brothers, William Kirkley, overman, John Foster, John Nicholson, Robert

A view of Burradon Colliery as depicted in the Illustrated London News *in 1860.* Author's collection. Inset: *The pit wheel erected as a memorial to those who died at Burradon.* Durham Mining Museum

Thompson and William Gascoigne proceeded inbye to see if anyone needed assistance. They had not got far when the effects of the afterdamp caused them to retreat.

Those on the bank had felt the force of the second explosion and had alerted the residents nearby. Miners who had been off duty were soon ready to descend the pit to search for survivors. The first two down were Robert Jefferson and Thomas Fryer. The latter had a son who was still underground but he was destined not to see him again. On getting a few hundred yards into the pit Jefferson and Fryer were both suffocated by the afterdamp. As the day wore on the crowd around the pit swelled into many hundreds and viewers and pitmen from other collieries arrived to assist in the rescue. The workings of the pit had suffered little serious damage so the main efforts were concentrated on restoring ventilation. To this end gallons of water were continuously poured down the shaft. An eleven-year-old trapper was the first body brought to bank followed by Alderson and his group. One of these men was still alive, although only barely, but he did survive. By late evening on Saturday fifty-six bodies had been recovered which were placed in open coffins that had been hastily put together in the colliery carpenters' shop. Once the bodies were identified they were taken to their respective homes. Throughout the process, because of the disfiguring injuries and burns to the bodies, some were wrongly identified which resulted in corpses being taken to the wrong homes and having to be moved again, causing further distress to the grieving families.

The plaque erected in thanks to D Little of Holywell Engineering for donating the Burradon pit wheel. Durham Mining Museum

Over half the valuable pit horses and ponies had also been killed and their bodies had to be removed as quickly as possible. The stench from their burnt hair and flesh would have been overpowering to those carrying out the underground recovery operation. This is how *The Times* reported the situation:

The joiners in the neighbourhood and those belonging to the pit were engaged all Friday night and Saturday in making coffins, a large pile of which were lying on the pit bank on Saturday. Two bodies were interred on Sunday, and the bodies of all the other unfortunate sufferers brought to bank would be buried yesterday. The village had a woeful appearance on Sunday, as large crowds flocked into it from the neighbouring towns and villages. The doors of the cottages where the dead were laid were mostly open; the cottages were scrupulously clean, the beds being hung with white linen, and the coffins were covered with linen of a similar quality. Each home, of course, where the dead were laid, told its own tale of sorrow. Numbers of friends of the bereaved reached the village on Sunday, and the day was one of the most melancholy that could be conceived.

The Times, 6 March

More bodies had been recovered by Monday and on Tuesday that of Benjamin Nicholson was found. The explorers knew that they were now near the source of the explosion as Nicholson's body had been torn to pieces. His remains had been scattered over a wide area and he was only identifiable by his cap. Nine more bodies were recovered that day which left three yet to be found. Ventilation was restored and on the evening of Wednesday, 7 March a shift was sent down to resume work. By 9 March the last three bodies had been found under a fall of stone which appeared to be the seat of the explosion.

The disaster left twenty-eight widows and eighty-eight children without a father and these were not the only ones to lose the breadwinner of the household. Thomas and John Marshall had supported four siblings and their widowed mother; John and George Thrift had been the sole support of their sister and grandparents; David Addy supported his aged mother as well as his wife; Thomas Lawson his widowed mother; William Nichol his parents and two siblings; Robert Jefferson as well as his wife and four children had also supported his widowed daughter and her two children. For four of the victims this had been their first day down Burradon Pit.

The dead were:

John Pease, 39, married, three children, father of John
John Pease, 10, son of John
Jacob Weatherley, 10
William Cook, 11
John Beadling, 11, cousin to Thomas
Thomas Beadling, 20, cousin to John
Daniel Duffy, 12
Edward Thompson, 14
William Wilkie, 49, married, three children, father of Thomas
Thomas Wilkie, 14, son of William
Thomas Grey, 15
John Hetherington, 15

The dedication plaque on the Burradon memorial. Durham Mining Museum

John Carr, 40, married, five children, father of Samuel
Samuel Carr, 15, son of John.
Thomas Marshall, 15, brother to John
John Marshall, 20, widowed mother, brother to Thomas
John Maddox, 15, brother to James and Thomas
James Maddox, 17, brother to John and Thomas
Thomas Maddox, 20, brother to John and James
George Thrift, 15, sister and grandparents, brother to John
John Thrift, 20, sister and grandparents, brother to George
Ritson Golightly, 15, brother to Thomas.
Thomas Golightly, 17, brother to Ritson
Isaac Johnson, 16
Henry Johnson, 17
Joseph Musgrave, 17
William Doxford, 16
Moses Thompson, 18, brother to Thomas
Thomas Thompson, 25, married, child, brother to Moses
James Nichol, 18
John Gallon, 18

Matthew Mordue, 20
Andrew Messer, 20, married
Matthew Hepplewhite, 20
John Carr, 21
John Fittes, 27
Thomas Fryer, 57, married, two children, father to Thomas
John Fryer, 21, son of Thomas
David Addy, 55, married
David Addy, 22, son of David, brother to John
John Addy, 24, son of David, brother to David
Thomas Dawson, 21.
James Hamor, 22, married, two children
John Jervis, 22
Thomas Lawson, 22
Francis Smith, 22
George Whips, 23, married, child
Thomas Phillips, 23, brother to David
David Phillips, 28, brother to Thomas
Ralph Herron, 23
Robert Kyle, 24, married, child
James Wood, 24
George Shotton, 25, married, two children
Martin Sankey, 25, married
William Nichol, 26, parents, two siblings
George Schimph, 26, married, child
Thomas Wilkinson, 29, married, child
George Fisher, 29, married
Edward Dryden, 29, married, child
William Donnelly, 30, married, two children
Alfred Allen, 30
John McWilliams, 30, married, three children
James Vought, 30
John Dewry, 31, married, three children
John Maddox, 31, married, five children
William Turner, 32, married, three children
Matthew Cleghorn, 33, married
Robert Leatham, 37, married, four children
James Brown, 38, married, three children
James Brown, 38, married, four children
William Alderson, 39, married, six children
Benjamin Nicholson, 43, married, seven children
Robert Soulsby, 45, married, three children
William Urwin, 45, married, five children
George Maddox, 46, married, six children
Robert Jefferson, 59, married, four children

Joseph Cowen junior acquired control of the Newcastle Chronicle *in 1859 and immediately aimed at selling his newspapers to the working man. He devoted a great deal of space to the industrial and political affairs of mining.* Author's collection

In 1860, the *Newcastle Courant* and *Newcastle Journal* were papers which supported the views of the business man and the rich while the *Weekly Chronicle* and the *Daily Chronicle* were for the working man. In 1859, the latter newspapers had been taken over by Joseph Cowen junior who was the son of an MP and a passionate supporter of the working man's rights. James Baxter Langley was the editor and devoted a considerable portion of newspaper space to the opinions and aspirations of the miners having become acquainted with the working men of the pits in the surrounding areas. Cowen and Langley now made a formidable team as champions of the working man. Langley had been supportive of the Miners' Provident Association which was to be set up with a central fund to be used to give relief to the sufferers of colliery accidents. Sadly, while the Miners' Association still existed in name only, some of those most involved in working towards its establishment died in the Burradon disaster three of whom were William Urwin, George Maddox and William Alderson.

The inquest was held before the coroner, Stephen Reed, who was mistrusted by the pitmen because he was believed to be biased towards the coal-owners. During the proceedings a plan of the colliery was produced that was supposed to illustrate the workings prior to the explosion. The plan showed a set of double doors that were placed close together so that if one were left open the other acted as a backup. Charles Carr was asked whether these doors had been in place prior to the explosion and he was forced to admit that there had only been a single door. It was suggested that adding double doors after the event was misleading but Carr insisted that a single door had been adequate and the second door had been added only as a precaution. He was also asked whether the workmen had complained to him about the ventilation and he replied that they had not. William Kirkley admitted to adding the doors to the plan three days after the explosion at the insistence of Carr but he also said that he did not believe the single door had anything to do with what had happened. Some of the pitmen stated that the ventilation had improved a little after Dunn's recommendations were acted upon. In January 1860, the air had once again become foul but they had not reported their concerns. A hewer, Williams, stated that on the morning

James Mather inspected Burradon pit after the explosion but his report was not read out at the inquest. Mather had assisted in the rescue attempts at St Hilda's Colliery in 1839. A strong advocate of the miners he successfully formed a committee to inquire into the causes of accidents in mines after the disaster at Hartley in 1862. Author's collection

81

of the disaster two blowers had ignited at his board. When asked why he had not reported it he said that they fired every day and the deputies were aware of it. The coroner suggested that if this had been reported the men that were using candles would have been issued instead with safety lamps. Williams disagreed that the officials would have taken this precaution. James Mather had inspected the pit after the explosion but Reed had refused to allow his report to be read out at the inquest. Both Mather's and the Mines Inspector's report were subsequently published in the *Daily Chronicle* – much to Reed's annoyance.

The coroner pointed out that the purpose of these inquests was to investigate the cause of death to the victims, not to find any particular person or body guilty. He had instructed the jury to sign a certificate to say that he had conducted the inquest with impartiality which was later condemned by Langley. In this case, however, the jury appear not to have been swayed by Reed's remarks and demands and decided that cause of death and apportion of blame went hand in hand. After many witness statements the jury's conclusion was that the accident was caused either by a fall or by a trapper's door being left open both of which would have affected the air-flow. They also suggested there had been some neglect or oversight on the part of some of the colliery officials and that the workmen were also at fault having not lodged a proper complaint on their concerns. It was further suggested that the inspection of the mines by Government officials was inadequate. But the jury's conclusions and even public opinion fell on deaf ears as far as Reed was concerned. If he had been in agreement it would have been a case of manslaughter which would have turned the industry on its head.

The final result was that the colliery owners were not found responsible for the disaster but even if they had been found wholly negligent it was unlikely whether any adequate compensation would have been paid to the widows and others in need of support. Joseph Bower, the owner of the colliery, paid for the funerals and offered £400 to aid the widows and orphans but this was nowhere near the amount that was needed. The pit-workers average yearly income at that time was about £31 and seventy-six wage earners had died. The general public were made aware of this through the newspapers and voices such as Langley, Cowen and Richard Fynes who was also a tireless campaigner for the miners.

An appeal in the *Newcastle Daily Chronicle* of 5 March read:

> Following the blackened and distorted remains to the miner's home reveals another scene less painful perhaps at the moment, but fraught with distressing fears for the future of old men and women and little helpless children. Empty regrets without Christian sympathising action is mere hypocrisy. The payments ought to be made as public compensations rather than as charity involving a deep sense of obligation on the part of the recipients.

Generosity was overwhelming and by April 1860 more than £2,000 in subscriptions and donations had been raised.

Richard Fynes, a champion of the pit-workers and author of a History of Northumberland and Durham Miners, *published in 1873.* Author's collection

Although the initial distribution of relief was a haphazard affair, eventually an Executive Committee was formed with seven men, one of whom was a pit-man that had been acquainted with many of the victims, Thomas Weatherly, who carried out the distribution of relief for many years following the disaster. In 1861, some of the cash that was raised was used to build a school. In 1884, the *Shields Daily News* printed an article which stated that the Burradon Fund was almost exhausted and there was to be a fund-raising event for the remaining seven widows of the victims.

(23) Pit: New Hartley

Location: Hartley, Northumberland
Type: Entombed
Fatalities: 204
Date: Thursday, 16 January 1862

> Puts for a headsman; makes about 4s. a day; has been down 6 years. The pit has made him sick and also to throw up his victuals many times, when he has to go home. Has had the headache very often; was never very strong but thinks he has the worse a good deal for the pit. Is now in wet places in the high seam; the water is over his ankles in many places. Gets sore feet many times. Reads easy words only. Cannot write at all. Goes to Sunday-school and chapel pretty often. (Looks very delicate)
>
> Robert Smith, aged 16, Hartley, 1841

According to the 1861 census the close-knit community of Hartley village had a population of 579. This figure was to be cut by over one third by the following year. This disaster was unique in both its cause and the fact that it had the highest number of fatalities of any prior

The mouth of the shaft at Hartley Colliery. Author's collection

or subsequent mine accident in North-East England or Cumberland and as such was to generate widespread public attention.

Coal had been mined from shallow pits at Hartley from the end of the thirteenth century. By the nineteenth century coal-owners were venturing to sink deeper and larger pits and in 1830 the shaft at Hartley was sunk eighty fathoms to three rich coal seams.

From 1847 the colliery was owned by the Carr family who had also bought Seghill, Burradon and Cowpen collieries about that time and still retained shares. The mine was subject to flooding and had been inundated in 1844. At the time the engineers thought that they had struck the sea. In 1845, the sinking of the Hester Pit began but again a problem was soon encountered when in 1852 water poured in flooding the shaft to a depth of 420 feet. The pump being used was obviously too small to do the job of clearing the mine so a new pumping engine was installed in about 1858, at the time the most powerful example in the north of England. The cylinders were immense and the cast-iron beam weighed forty-two tons. Even so, water was still a problem in the mine and it was only when they holed into the workings of the abandoned Mill Pit did the water become less of a problem.

The pit was worked by means of one shaft although there was a staple from the surface to High Main and one from the Yard to the High Main. The shaft was twelve feet in diameter with three inch planking forming the brattice down the centre. The Low Main was accessible only by the shaft which was bratticed down the middle. The enormous beam of the pumping engine was anchored in the engine-house with the arm reaching over the shaft working in a see-sawing motion to raise and return the rods which operated the water-raising mechanism that was all the way down the shaft.

The day of the tragedy started out as any other with the fore-shift already in the pit and the back-shift beginning to leave. Sixteen men had already been brought to bank and the cage was being drawn up with a further eight occupants when, as it was about halfway, the unthinkable happened. Without warning the great beam poised over the shaft broke, shattering everything on its downward path. Two of the four iron chains that supported

Thomas Watson, pitman, was one of three men who survived the Hartley disaster after the wrecking of the cage trapped them in the shaft. He later testified at the inquest. Author's collection

the cage snapped, sending half of the cage and four of its human cargo down the shaft. Thomas Watson, William Sharp, Ralph Robinson and George Sharp were left clinging to what remained of the cage, the latter person with a severely injured leg. To make their hold even more precarious the pipes had fractured causing water to pour down on them. There was a cry from below and George Sharp recognised his son's voice. Watson somehow managed to climb down the treacherous sixty feet or so to reach the injured youth. He found that Robert Bewick was also alive but both he and young Sharp were critically injured. Watson could do nothing for them so they prayed and sang a hymn. Watson was exhausted and numb, with the cold seeping through his saturated clothes. He did not know how long it had been since the accident but certainly hours when his two injured comrades drew their last breath. Eventually, through the efforts of John Short, engine-wright of the colliery, a rope was sent down with a lantern attached. A loop followed to raise the men still clinging to the cage but George Sharp was weary and in too much pain from his injured leg to hold on. He fell not far from where Watson was standing and was killed on impact. The other two men and Watson eventually reached safety twelve hours after the cage fell. Watson's wife had died in childbirth five months before leaving him with four motherless children so his survival was truly a miracle.

When the beam broke the huge mass of cast-iron had hit the brattice with terrific force which caused the wood and iron framework to hurtle to the bottom of the shaft blocking the only means of escape to those still underground. The *Newcastle Daily Chronicle* described the pit-top scene:

The flaming beacons on the high platform of Hartley Pit glared steadily in the eyes of weary-footed pedestrians approaching from Deleval or from nearer cottages. A thin cover of snow overspread the ground, and had changed the dark dry brown of the coaly roadways to a path of clear whiteness. The pit-heaps are ashy grey and the stillness of death reined around, broken only by the interminable orders for the gin, the crab, and the jack, which is heard through the morning air. Black figures bent their steps noiselessly towards the gleaming fires, where groups of persons were sitting or reclining quietly, the fountains of their grief being well nigh exhausted, and the anguish

The image depicts the broken beam of the pumping engine at Hartley Colliery. It was this which caused the disaster in 1862. www.chmrc.co.uk

William Coulson, pit-sinker, used his forty-eight years of experience to supervise the rescue attempts at Hartley. Author's collection

Robert Turnbull, one of the men who devoted his time giving assistance wherever he could at Hartley during the attempts at rescue. Author's collection

of their minds, great as it is, being almost overpowered by the sleepy influences of the hour. Around the pit's mouth, however, eager spectators still watched the indications of the progress of the work, as if at any moment friends might be brought to bank whose lives depended on their presence at the moment of arrival. Meanwhile the ponderous machinery worked smoothly on; the ropes, as thick as a man's leg, glided up and down like greasy, slimy serpents, and in the hollow depths of the pit the lights burnt distinctly in a watery atmosphere.

David Wilkinson, George Emmerson and William Shields were all pit-sinkers who displayed courage and fortitude throughout the rescue attempts at Hartley. Author's collection

In other disasters it would have been the fellow workers of the victims that would volunteer to assist in rescue attempts but in this instance almost the whole workforce were the victims. However, no effort was spared with men from all over the North-East giving their expertise to try and reach the trapped men. William Coulson, who was an experienced pit-sinker without equal in his field was put in charge of the rescue operation. He and his heroic teams worked tirelessly to clear the debris and place supports where they were required. Although the trapped men would be hungry and thirsty four days into the operation there was still a strong belief that they would survive. On Monday night this belief was to turn into despair when the sinkers began to suffer nausea and sickness, the effects of noxious gas. On Tuesday morning this was confirmed when a large volume of gas was released as some timber was cleared away. The rescue had to cease as further efforts would have resulted in the deaths of the rescuers. On Wednesday, two of the sinkers, Richard and Thomas Boyd, covering their faces against the poisonous fumes, squeezed through a small hole and went a little way in to see first two then more and more bodies. On their return to bank both men had to be given tea and brandy before they could speak. They had been affected by the bad air and also, no doubt, by what they had seen. When they did manage to speak to the waiting crowds it was to dash all hope that any of those entombed would be brought out alive. One can only imagine the moment for those trapped victims when the last glimmer of hope of a rescue faded. The more robust would have survived the longest and must have felt a mixture of fear, sorrow and despair as they watched their comrades die around them.

All that was now left for the rescuers was to concentrate on removing the bad air and restore a fresh current into the workings so that the bodies could be recovered.

A local paper printed the following report:

At half-past 4 o'clock the intelligence of the discovery of the bodies was conveyed to the village. It is impossible in the limits of language to convey an idea of the terrible scenes in every house of this doomed village. Every house of mourning, and that is every one, is filled with sympathizing friends and acquaintances, and the ministering hand of woman is busy in affording consolation to these unhappy women – now too surely widows. In every house may be heard the hysterical sob, the agonized wail of suffering woman, weeping for the husband of her love and the father of her orphan children, now lying cold and silent in the depths of the fatal pit. It is also peculiarly painful to hear the wailings of tender infants whose mothers are too sorrow-stricken to attend to their wants. The street of the village is filled with women who steal noiselessly from house to house on their mission of mercy, endeavouring, by arts only known to woman, to impart solace to these bereaved ones.

George Baker Forster was destined to become a clergyman after graduating with an MA but changed his career course by becoming a mining engineer. He took a prominent part in endeavouring to clear the shaft after the disaster at Hartley in 1862. Afterwards he became very involved in public matters concerned with collieries. Author's collection

William Shields was one of the leading sinkers involved with the attempt at rescue. For his efforts he received £30 and a Silver Medal. Courtesy of Dimity Pollard (nee Shields)

William Shields' wife Margaret who must have suffered an agonising wait as her husband carried out his dangerous task. Courtesy of Dimity Pollard (nee Shields)

So they have been, so they are, and so they will doubtless remain to the end of time. Not women alone, however, are engaged in this hallowed mission, for a few ministers of the gospel may be seen, hurrying to and fro, in the semi-darkness, engaged in the work of their Master, and endeavouring, by their spiritual consolation, to cheer the 'weary and heavy laden.' It is scarcely possible to conceive a more sorrowful scene, and it is heartrending to reflect that every house is tenanted by grief-stricken widows and fatherless children, many of them left fatherless at the very threshold of the battle of life, and deprived, at one fell swoop, of the hand that should have guarded their infant years. May He who tempers the wind to the shorn lamb be their solace and stay in this their hour of adversity! In our hurried passage along the street many scenes came under our notice almost too sacred for us even to allude to – here the weeping mother spasmodically pressing the crowing infant to her breast, who was lisping out the name of its 'dada,' and a gush of tears and a hopeless shake of the head told too truly that the heart of that loved 'dada' was cold in death at the bottom of the mine. There might be seen a fine little boy sobbing as if his heart would break, and looking wistfully towards the pit, as if he expected to see some well-remembered form, and perhaps wondering, poor little fellow, what his unhappy mother meant by telling him he was an orphan. There, too, might be seen an aged and infirm man, with his grey hair tossed to and fro by the wintry blast, endeavouring to comfort his little grand

daughter, whose outstretched hand was pointed towards the spot where her father was wont to work, and who eagerly scanned the countenance of every passer-by, in the hope, probably, of recognizing her long absent father. That father is now cut off from all earthly ties, and is now 'where the wicked cease from troubling and the weary are at rest'.

From Saturday morning body after body was fastened in a sling, brought to the surface and coffined. It took seventeen and a half hours to complete the terrible task of bringing 199 bodies out of the pit. All the bodies recovered had been in the vicinity of the shaft so a further search of the workings was made in case there were others. Eventually the explorers came to about ten feet of water which meant the Low Main seam was flooded which put an end to the search. Forty-three pit-ponies had also perished. Robert Turnbull faced the waiting crowd and had the unenviable task of announcing the name of each of the dead as they were identified and placed in their coffin. Richard Fynes recorded this observation:

When the names of the bodies rescued were announced, it was painfully interesting to watch the feeling of exultation which took possession of some of the poor creatures waiting for the cold forms of their husbands, their sons, or lovers; for though hope had left their breasts they still seemed to feel some relief in having the inanimate bodies of their loved ones restored to them. They were dead, it was true, but they had them once more beside them, dead though they were, and even this was a joy in their great affliction. In all the large village of Hartley there was scarcely a house into which death had not been introduced; whilst in some there were two, three, four, and even five dead forms laid out. It is idle to write of the grief which prevailed, for no writer can adequately describe the universal mourning which took possession of the whole community.

Scratched and chalked messages written by the victims were found, in some cases perhaps giving some solace to their families. Within the tragedy lay other personal tragedies such as John Bewick's thirty-three-year-old wife who was extremely ill with consumption. When she was told of his death it sounded her death knell also and she was interred along with him leaving five orphaned children between the ages of two and eleven. Robert McMullin's wife was also ill and she died soon after the disaster leaving an infant daughter. John Ainsley was the support of his parents, John and Elizabeth, who were both blind. For George Hindmarch, John Coyle and Harry Clough this had been their first, and last, shift in Hartley Pit. William Smith was not working in the pit but had merely gone down to have a look around. Patrick Walpole, aged 30, left a wife from which payment of relief was withheld. This was the only one of the sufferers to which this happened. No reason was given.

The consecrated ground at St Alban's church at Earsdon was not large enough to accommodate so many burials as the victims of the Burradon disaster had been interred there just two years previously. A field adjoining was given by the Duke of Northumberland for the sorrowful purpose. One can now only imagine the sight of the grave-diggers toiling in the backdrop of the church to excavate the earth for 204 coffins, some to single and others to multiple graves. T Wemyss Reid was a reporter for the *Newcastle Daily Journal* and had

The Illustrated London News *published this image showing the coffins leaving Colliery Row for Earsdon churchyard. It was reported that at one point the procession was four miles long.* www.chmrc.co.uk

Because Earsdon parish churchyard did not have room for the interment of so many bodies an adjacent field was given by the Duke of Northumberland. The trenches were of different sizes as family members were buried together with the largest holding thirty-three coffins. www.chmrc.co.uk

been on the scene throughout the whole event. His reports have left a lasting graphic account of what took place. One of his last tasks was to accompany the mourners as they buried their dead of which he wrote:

> When the solemn words, 'Ashes to ashes and dust to dust' were being uttered, darkness had well nigh fallen upon the awful scene. And the indescribable feeling of awe which the thought of being in the midst of so many unburied human remains occasioned, and from which the spectator was separated by a few feet of space and a few thin deal boards, was intensified by the falling gloom of the evening.

A list of the victims and those they left behind follows:

John Ainsley, 19, parents
William Alderton, 31, wife, two children
William Allan, 36, wife, five children
James Amour, 48, wife, four children, father of Richard
Richard Amour, 14, son of James
William Anderson, 17
John Armstrong, 36, wife, two children, father of Edward and John
Edward Armstrong, 12, son of John
John Armstrong, 10, son of John
Adam Atkinson, 20, wife, four children
William Bannan 24
Mark Bell, 23
Thomas Bell, 23
Thomas Bell, 13, widowed mother, five siblings
John Bennett, 25, wife
James Bewick, 34, pregnant wife, two daughters, brother to John
John Bewick, 32, wife, five children, brother to James
Robert Bewick, 30, wife, three children
Samuel Birtley, 24, pregnant wife, child, baby born four days after the disaster

Samuel Blackburn, 26, wife, child
John Broadfoot, 19
Thomas Brown, 25, wife, son, brother to Ralph
Ralph Brown, 15, brother to Thomas
George Brown, 31, pregnant wife, two children
William Brown, 25, wife, two children
John Burn, 52, wife, three children, father of Thomas
Thomas Burn, 18, son of John
James Campbell, 28, wife, three children
George Carling, 27, wife, four children
Thomas B Chambers, 55, wife, ill daughter, father of Clark
Clark Chambers, 19, son of Thomas
Alfred Cheetham, 33, wife, two children
Henry Clough, 47, wife, three children
John Coyle, 28
Thomas Coal, 37, wife, five children
John Coulson, 33, wife, four children
Robert Coulson, 26, wife, three children
John Cousins, 18, brother to Robert
Robert Cousins, 12, brother to John
Philip Cross, 59, wife, two children, widowed daughter with two children
Philip Cross, 20, son of Philip
John Davidson, 38, wife, three children, father of William
William George Davidson, 11, son of John
Thomas Dawson, 49, wife, four children, father of John
John Dawson, 12, son of Thomas
Robert Dixon, 12, mother, two siblings, father was in a lunatic asylum
William Dixon, 27, wife, two children
William Dixon, 34, single with a son
John Douglas, 25, wife, adopted child
Patrick Duffy, 34, wife, three children, father of James
James Duffy, 10, son of Patrick.
Allison Elliott, 29, wife, two children
Edward Elliott, 19
William Fairburn, 70, ill wife, father of George
George Fairburn, 33, son of William.
Henry Ford, 32, pregnant wife, brother to John
John Ford, 27, pregnant wife, a child, brother to Henry
Peter Ford, 12, ill father, two siblings
Joseph Foster, 18, brother to John
John Foster, 15, brother to Joseph
George Fulton, 25, pregnant wife
John Gallagher, 32, wife, two children, brother to Duncan
Duncan Gallagher, 28, brother to John
Henry Gibson, 18 years
William Gledson, 71, wife, father of Thomas and George
George Gledson, 41, wife, child, son of William

Thomas Gledson, 36, wife, son of William, father of Thomas
Thomas Gledson, 16, son of Thomas
William Gledson, 43, wife, child
Oswald Gleghorn, 24, wife, three children
James Glen, 18, disabled father, brother to William and George
William Glen, 14, disabled father, brother to James and George
George Glen, 12, disabled father, brother to James and William
Patrick Gormerley, 25
Christopher Graham, 27, wife, two children
George Hall, 28, wife, two children
James Hamelton, 56, wife, child, father of James
James Hamelton, 12, son of James
John Harding, 15
Thomas Harrison, 16
Frank Hauxwell, 25, wife, child
George Hays, 41, wife, three children
Thomas Hepple, 27
George Hill, 31, wife, three children, one in the Blind Asylum
Robert Hill, 21
George Hindmarch, 30, wife, five children
John Hodge, 33, wife, three children
Andrew Houston, 34, wife, eight day old baby
George Howard, 20
Joseph Humble, 27
Peter Hammel, 33, wife, two children
Henry Hunter, 13
Winship Jack/Jacques, 24, wife, three children
Joseph Johnson, 41, wife, three children, brother to Robert
Robert Johnson, 42, brother to Joseph
William Kennedy, 30, pregnant wife, two children, baby born four days after the disaster
George Laws, 20, widowed mother
Thomas Laws, 34, widowed mother
John Liddle, 46, wife, four children, father of John, George and Thomas
John Liddle, 11, son of John
George Liddle, 16, son of John
Thomas Liddle, 18, son of John
Thomas Liddle, 41, wife, three children, brother to John, father of Thomas
Thomas Liddle, 11, son of Thomas
William Liddle, 40, wife, four children, father of James and William
James Liddle, 15, son of William
William Liddle, 17, son of William
William Louce, 30, pregnant wife, five children
John Long, 15, cousin to Robert
Robert Long, 17, cousin to John
Thomas Macauley, 38, wife
Richard McClutchey, 24, pregnant wife, three children
William McCrachen, 24

William McFarlane, 15
John McKee, 55, pregnant wife, three children, father of Adam
Adam McKee, 24, son of John
Hugh Mason, 24
Robert McMullin, 27, ill wife, infant daughter
Walter Miller, 43, wife, five children, brother to William
William Miller, 34, wife, three children, brother to Walter
Andrew Morgan, 44, daughter
John Mullon, 36, wife, four children
Robert Murley, 26, wife
Michael Murray, 26
Peter Manderson, 50, wife, uncle to Peter Nesbit
Peter Nesbit, 20, nephew to Peter Manderson
John Nicholson, 14, brother to Joseph
Joseph Nicholson, 21, brother to John
Joshua Nicholson, 52, wife, three children
Robert North, 26, wife, two children
John North, 12, brother to George and Alexander
George North, 15, brother to John and Alexander
Alexander North, 10, brother to John and George
William Oliver, 56, wife, daughter, father to John, James, William and Peter
Peter Oliver, 15, son of William
William Oliver, 17, son of William
James Oliver, 21, son of William
John Oliver, 27, son of William
John Ormston, 32, wife, two children
William Palmer, 35, wife, three children
William Pape, 14
Thomas Pearson, 28
William Redpath, 24, pregnant wife, three children
Robert Randall, 33, wife, five children
Alexander Richardson, 22, wife
Hugh Riley, 30, wife, two children
Matthew Robinson, 30, wife, two children
Thomas Robinson, 42, wife, three children
Ralph Robson, 36, pregnant wife, five children
James Robson, 12, disabled father
Thomas Ross, 46, daughter
Edward Rowley, 33, wife, three children
John Rutherford, 25, brother to William
William Rutherford, 23, brother to John
Thomas Rutherford, 32, wife, two children
George Scurfield, 51, aged parents, sibling who took fits
Thomas Sebastian, 19, widowed mother
George Sharp, 49, wife, three children, father of Johnson and George
Johnson Sharp, 13, son of George
George Sharp, 15, son of George

Henry Sharp, 44, wife, brother to Thomas
Thomas C Sharp, 48, brother to Henry
Patrick Sherlock, 28
George Skinner, 14
Robert Small, 19
Frank Smith, 33, wife, five children.
William Smith, 19, pregnant wife
Edward Softley, 17
Eli Stainsby, 23
William Stanley, 34
Joseph Taylor, 36, pregnant wife, two children
William Telford, 29, pregnant wife, two children
John Ternent, 44, four or five children, father of George
George Ternent, 15, son of John
William Ternent, 40
George Thirlwell, 27, wife, two children
William Tibbs, 32, wife, four children
James Tryer, 36
John Veitch, 21
George Wade, 31, wife, infant son
Benjamin Walker, 21
William Walker, 12, widowed mother, brother to James
James Terney, 14
James Walker, 16, brother to William
Patrick Walpool, 30, wife
John Wanless, 15, brother to Thomas and Christopher, brother-in-law to Wanless Jack
Thomas Wanless, 19, brother to John and Christopher, brother-in-law to Wanless Jack
Christopher Wanless, 20, brother to John and Thomas, brother-in-law to Wanless Jack
Thomas Watson, 30
Thomas Watson, 31
James Watson, 38, wife
John Watson, 39, wife, four children
Joseph Watson, 16
Thomas Weirs, 40, wife, four children
Robert Weirs, 20
George Wilson, 38
William Wilson, 16
William Wilson, 12
John Wilkinson, 23
David Wypher, 24, pregnant wife, mentally retarded son
William White, 16, widowed mother
John Young, 25, wife, two children
John Youll, 28, wife, four children
Henry Younger, 33

The verdict at the conclusion of the inquest was that the victims had met their deaths 'by accident'. The coroner, Stephen Reed, praised those who showed outstanding courage in

The Hartley Disaster Medal was awarded to those who risked their lives in the rescue attempt. The medals were all silver other than that awarded to William Coulson which was gold. These men also received a monetary reward for their efforts. Author's collection

trying to save victims. He suggested that in future the beams of colliery engines should be of malleable iron instead of cast metal.

If there had been two shafts at Hartley, except for those that fell from the cage, there would have been no further deaths as those below would have been able to exit the mine by a second shaft. James Mather was born in Newcastle and had studied medicine and philosophy at the University of Edinburgh. His name comes up as being on the scene to assist after numerous disasters and of seeking the cause. After Hartley a meeting of what was described as 'resolute body of men' took place in Newcastle to launch a Relief Fund but then went on to discuss the appalling number of recent fatalities in the pits. Mather made a powerful thought provoking speech concerning all the disasters and pointing out the dire need for changes in the system. The one light that shone after that dark day at Hartley was that the voices of Mather and others were heard and legislature was introduced forcing the coal-owners of new or established pits to install two shafts.

An extract from a poem by George Cooke entitled *The Hartley Calamity* seems apt:

Ten score lives have proved it true
The one-shaft system will not do
The horrid system one way out
Has slain its hundreds there's no doubt
May Hartley in the memory live
A death-blow to the system give.

There were hundreds of letters of support and condolence to the victims' families including correspondence from Queen Victoria who was also in mourning having become a widow on 14 December 1861. But more than sympathy was needed for the grieving families. Almost

The headstone dedicated to William and Margaret Shields in Cowpen Cemetery, Blyth. Under William's name are the words 'Master Sinker of Blyth'. Courtesy of Dimity Pollard (nee Shields)

the entire male working population of the village had been wiped out leaving hundreds without any means of support. The disaster must have touched the very heart of Victorian society as within the space of just three months the relief fund had reached £70,000 with the final total a staggering £82,000. The sum of 7s per week was assigned to each widow and 10s 6d to a widow and child, 13s 6d for a widow and 2 children, 15s 6d for a widow and three children, 17s 6d for a widow and 4 children, 19s 6d for a widow and five children. The allowances would continue with no misconduct on the widow's part as long as they remained unmarried and the children to age fifteen years for girls and twelve years for boys. Infirm adults received 7s per week. The widows would get £20 on remarrying and £3 for funeral expenses on dying with £1 for the death of a child. By 1880, there were still sixty-nine recipients of relief from the fund, twenty-three of whom were widows.

The *Newcastle Courant* on 23 May 1862 listed the men that were named as heroes for their part in the rescue attempt:

William Coulson	Matthew Chapman
William Coulson junior	Edward Davison
George Emmerson	Matthew Dodds
William Shields	George Graham
David Wilkinson	John Henderson
John Angus	Thomas Hetherington
John Burns	Ralph Harrison
Mitchell Bailey	Robert Hamilton
Fenwick Charlton	John Heron

Eldon Heron	James Muters
Ralph Heron	John Nevins
Lashley Hope	George Pace
William Johnson	William Reed
Richard Johnson	John Smith
Peter Lindsay	Henry Snowden
John Little	John Sedgwick
R Maughan	Andrew Swaine
John Manderson	Jesse Smith
Robert Milburne	Robert Wilson

A special fund was set up to recognise the heroic actions of those that had taken part in the rescue attempts. Donations were received from all over the country and the final sum set aside was £1,587. Commemorative medals were struck with Coulson, as the leader, being awarded gold and the others silver. The remaining balance of the fund was divided and presented according to the amount of time each man had spent in the shaft. No amount was stated for William Coulson senior and junior; Emmerson, Shields and Wilkinson received £30 each and the others received from £19 down to £4. The silver medal awarded to William Shields was donated by his grandson, Major Harry Shields, to the Northumberland National Union of Mine Workers and is located in a cabinet at the Miners' Union Office in Newcastle.

It was to be 1900 before the seam was eventually drained and the death-trap of so many re-entered. According to those who first entered, the tubs and gear were found as if standing ready for work to begin and the hewers' picks still where they had been hurriedly abandoned to lie gradually corroding for thirty-eight years.

The impressive memorial dedicated to the 204 men and boys that died in New Hartley Pit in 1862 was paid for by public subscription and erected in St Alban's parish churchyard. Author's collection

(24) Pit: Walker

Location: Walker, Northumberland
Type: Explosion
Fatalities: 16
Date: Saturday, 22 November 1862

The Walker Colliery, owned in 1862 by Lambert, Nicholson and Company, was one of the few in the district into which water had not burst. Ventilation was provided by two furnaces in the centre of the colliery and the pit had a good reputation for safety among the colliers. Davy lamps were used and no naked lights were permitted. The pit employed about 120 hewers and another eighty or so who worked on the haulage and at the surface. Just previous to the explosion a 'trouble' had been encountered. This was the local term for a mass of stone within the coal seam and the usual practice was to blast the stone away to reach the coal on the other side. All the men employed on the first shift came up at 4pm on Friday and on any other day would have gone to work on the following morning but that Saturday was their fortnightly pay day and, as was the practice, the pit was not worked.

The miners and their families were looking forward to a large Sunday school tea-party that was to be held on Saturday night. When there were no hewers at work stonemen and shifters were sent down to do necessary repairs and odd jobs. At 2am on the Saturday morning a group of twenty-eight of these 'off-hands', as they were known, began their shift. There were also nine horses and twenty-one ponies in the underground stables. Between 5 and 6am three men who were working near the shaft heard a loud 'whooshing' noise and were hit by a wind that knocked them to the ground. At the same time Charles Robson and Joseph Richardson, two of the banksmen, heard a noise which they described as sounding like a muffled report of a boiler explosion. At the same time straw, particles of coal and debris blew out of the shaft. The whole episode only lasted a very short time and everything then settled back to normal. They immediately informed Charles Cooper, the engineman,

Grief stricken women identify the bodies of their loved ones. Author's collection

of what had taken place and he in turn sent word to William Cole, the resident viewer. The three men nearest to the shaft had managed to get into the cage and were drawn up uninjured but in shock and suffering slight effects from afterdamp. Several explorers descended the pit where a further eight men and a boy were found alive. All were hurriedly taken from the pit and given medical attention. Some had been more badly affected by the noxious gas than others but all eventually recovered.

By Sunday night sixteen bodies had been recovered. Those nearest the 'trouble' were badly burned and some had sustained injuries by being thrown for a considerable distance. The remainder had died of suffocation from the afterdamp. When a watch was removed from the body of George Barnes it was found it had stopped at 6.10 which established the exact time of the explosion.

The hay had been set alight in the stables and, with no means of escape, all the horses and ponies except one had perished. A little pony, French, who had been at other collieries prior to Walker was found frightened but uninjured. He was taken to bank where a considerable fuss was made of him. The fire was soon extinguished using buckets of water and, other than the stables, there was little damage to the pit and with a few repairs it was up and running within a couple of days.

The victims and those left in need of support were:

George Mitford, 'young man'
William Burrell, young man
Joseph Atkinson, brother to Thomas
Thomas Atkinson, brother to Joseph
William Barnes, wife, three children, brother to George
George Barnes, 47, wife, four children, brother to William
John Elerton, dependant widowed mother
Martin Fatkin, wife, two adult children
John Forster, wife, three adult children
James Haswell, wife, two dependants and one adult child
John Holt, wife, child
Kenny Thomas, wife, three children
Thomas Miller, dependant widowed mother
John Mitcheson, wife, two children
John Moore, wife
George Watson, 'motherless child'

The dependants of the victims were not provided for as the men at Walker Colliery were not in a Permanent Relief Fund.

The inquest was held before Stephen Reed, the coroner for South Northumberland, at the Railway Inn, Walker. There were only a few workmen present and only three gave evidence. It was thought that others had stayed away in fear of losing their jobs. Inspector of Mines, Matthias Dunn, had no legal advisor present and, although there were a few colliery viewers around the coroner's chair, none assisted Dunn. He believed the ventilation was not up to scratch, especially when the furnace was not working at its full capacity as was the case on the day of the explosion. Statements from the viewers admitted that there was the presence of gas but they insisted there had not been enough to be dangerous. No-one was able to pinpoint the cause of the explosion with certainty and the conclusion was a verdict of accidental death. What follows is an extract from a letter to the editor which was published in *The Times* on the day following the release of the results of the inquest:

I learn that the verdict of the inquest connected with the recent explosion at the Walker Colliery, is 'explosion purely accidental'. I have carefully studied the report of this inquest in your columns, and am puzzled to understand how such a definite verdict should have been recorded. Experienced men, it is stated, 'very minutely' examined the workings after the disaster, and were not able to discover where or how the explosion originated. The ventilation was declared to be ample. Nevertheless, it is certain that firedamp had accumulated in one part of the pit in sufficient volume to produce an explosive mixture, whether by slow leakage from the coal or, as sometimes happens, by sudden irruption. It is also clear that in this case there must have been a naked light of some kind with which the gas came into contact. One viewer expresses his opinion that ignition may have been due to a defective or injured safety-lamp. I need hardly observe that the gas called firedamp is not spontaneously inflammable for, if it were, safety-lamps would be useless. It was given in evidence that from the appearances in the locality where the men had been blasting the explosion did not occur there; and in support of this conclusion was adduced 'the fact of the lamps of the deputies who were working there having been found with their tops on and all secure'. Now, where blasting is carried on there must be fuses, and these fuses must be lit; but it is to be presumed that safety-lamps are not allowed to be opened for this purpose. The Lucifer match is a very convenient and obvious source of light in such cases, and, unless it could be shown that there were no matches underground, the evidence of the satisfactory condition of the safety-lamps found near the site of the blasting operations affords no indication whatever that the explosion did not take place in that part of the pit. The inquest has not thrown any light on the cause of the accident, and a more reasonable verdict would have been 'death by explosion, of which the cause is unknown'. The verdict, as it stands, exonerates all persons from blame, dead or alive. But a naked light there must have been in this pit, in which the safety-lamp was considered essential to the protection of life. What was that light? A defective safety-

A hewer at work. Author's collection

lamp would imply culpable negligence, and so would the use of Lucifer matches in a pit where naked lights were strictly forbidden. The explosion may have been purely accidental, but, assuredly, no evidence was advanced at the inquest to prove that it was.

The majority of the inquests that were held to establish cause of death in the mines appear to be almost farcical as it was a rare occurrence when blame was laid at the feet of the coal-owners or colliery officials. On occasions a disaster would be attributed to an individual who had lost his life and was unable to dispute the findings. Letters such as the above were becoming more frequent which shows that the general public were gradually taking more notice of the proceedings and voicing strong opinions while asking for answers.

(25) Pit: Coxlodge

Location: Coxlodge, Northumberland
Type: Explosion
Fatalities: 20
Date: Friday, 6 March 1863

> All work the same hours, from a little before 6 till about 6 and after in the evening. Many of them having some distance to go do not get home before 7 and 8 o'clock. It is very often 7 before they come up the pit, as they loose the work at half-past 6 and some have to walk more than a mile, or 2 miles sometimes, to the bottom of the shaft; and so it is sometimes they get up the pit. Four boys have worked once a double shift, 24 hours without coming up the pit. John Forster, aged 13, had his leg broken by slipping his hold of the rope when he was going down the pit and he fell to the bottom, and was off 20 weeks. Not lame now. John Trahan had the rolleys run over him at Wreckington and was off 2 months with a bruised leg. Has been often off from sickness and head-aching, and so on. Was not strong before he was in pits. Eight other boys have had slighter accidents at times. Ten boys can read easy words. Four boys write their names. Fourteen attend Sunday-schools pretty often. Five attend worship mostly. None attend a night-school. Three or four complain of the headache and sickness sometimes from bad air, etc.
>
> Evidence given to the Children's Employment Commission in 1841 regarding sixteen boys aged between 10 and 14 working at Coxlodge Colliery.

Coxlodge Colliery had been opened prior to 1821 and by 1863 was owned by Joshua Bower of Leeds. It was about ninety-five fathoms deep and had the required two shafts. Both safety lamps and naked lights were used. In 1844, during a previous ownership, the colliery had fired three times within a month causing three deaths and injury to more than ten persons. William Maddison was employed as the manager in 1860 and had made improvements to the ventilation though obviously not of a sufficiency to avert an accident.

On the morning of the disaster there were twenty-five men and boys working about two miles inbye from the shaft. When they heard the explosion eight of the men tried to get back to the shaft by their usual route but they were beaten back by afterdamp. They came upon a stopping that had been blown out and six of the group ran off. Joshua Turner and James

An etching by Thomas H Hair depicting the Jubilee Pit at Coxlodge in 1844. Author's collection

Richardson, who had a lamp, stayed together and wandered about for some time before they eventually found their way out. William Hann, a deputy, and Ralph Cowley also met the afterdamp and had to use another route which took them back past the bodies of their comrades.

A rescue operation was soon underway and seven miners were brought from the pit alive. Father and Son Robert and Michael Bell died soon after from burns. Robert Stonehouse, nineteen-year-old William Walton, Edward Ramsey, a boy, William Kenrick and Thomas Hooper, remained according to the medical attendants 'in a somewhat precarious state'.

The inquest was commenced to establish cause of death on nineteen victims but Thomas Hooper did not survive and it is probable that others of the injured died later. The following is a list of the twenty known victims:

Robert Hutton, 12, driver
Matthew Short, 13, driver
Robert Maughan, 13, driver
William Reed, 13
Joseph Waugh, 14, driver
George Ramsay, 14, driver
Robert Wealens, 15, driver
George Pattison, 16, driver
William Harrison, 16, drawer
Robert Hann, 16, driver

Michael Bell, 17, hewer, son of Robert
Robert Bell, 37, hewer, married, five or six children, father of Michael
Isaac Bambrough, 18, flat boy
Thomas Nichol, 19, hewer
Thomas Patterson, 19, putter
Mark Simpson, 20, putter
Robert Rowell, 21, hewer
David Mole, 31, hewer, married, two children
Thomas Baker, 36, hewer, married, two children
Thomas Hooper

The inquest took place at the Brandling Arms Inn, Bulmans Village before the coroner, Stephen Reed. The room was filled with miners and others who were interested including relatives who had lost loved ones in the explosion. The first witness called was William Maddison, the head viewer of the colliery who told the court that the mine was worked with naked lights and safety lamps and he thought the ventilation of the mine adequate and had never had any complaints from the men. There were approved rules displayed in the colliery office and the men who wanted them had copies. He was down the pit on the Monday before the accident and examined the whole of the workings and found them safe. Matthias Dunn had inspected the pit after the disaster and considered that the gas had escaped from an old bord at the top and fired at a candle in the northern most bord where shot-firing had been taking place. George Turnbull, a deputy at the colliery, was then called. The coroner questioned him on the safety of shot-firing in the mine and he answered that

The Regent Pit at Coxlodge from an etching by Thomas H Hair in 1844. Nineteen perished here in 1863. Author's collection

the men got more coal in less time with less labour. The coroner then commented: 'Well you are there to give information but I can give my own opinion, and I think it would be better for the men and owners to be content with less coal rather than run the risk of firing shots.'

A hewer who had worked at the colliery for twenty-six years stated that he believed the ventilation to be defective and shot-firing extremely dangerous. The final witness was mining engineer Thomas Emmerson Forster who had been requested by the owners to make an inspection of the colliery after the disaster. His conclusion was that Bell's place had holed into an old bord that had been partially filled with rubbish and the gas that had lodged there had fired at Bell's candle.

Coroner Reed, was at this time well into his seventies and, in what was to be his final public statement, he summed up the evidence. Addressing the jury, he said what they had to consider was:

> If they thought that there was any negligence on the part of the management of that colliery, or if anything was wanting, the only thing he could say was, that the deputy at the time had it in his power to withdraw the men. They would consider whether there was any want of attention on his part whether there was a purely accidental occurrence which no foresight could prevent.

He added that in his judgement the use of candles and smoking underground should be banned. After hearing his speech the jury retired for about five minutes and the foreman gave the following verdict:

> That David Moore and eighteen others on the 16th of March were accidentally killed in an explosion of gas in the Leonard's Cross Cut district of the Coxlodge Colliery and they recommend that the use of naked lights be discontinued.

The officials were again exonerated from any blame. Later, in *Local Records,* Thomas Fordyce wrote of the disaster:

> One of the most remarkable things in connection with this sad occurrence was the very slight amount of attention, on the part of the public, which it had attracted. The inhabitants of this district seemed to have their appetites for horrors of this description completely surfeited, and the consequence was, that the scene of the calamity had scarcely been visited by anyone, nor had the catastrophe caused a sensation even in the immediate neighbourhood of the spot.

As most of the victims were young men or boys there were three widows and about ten children left without support. Sadly, this relatively small number of victims would not have made headline news for long.

(26) Pit: Seghill

Location: Seghill, Northumberland
Type: Explosion
Fatalities: 7
Date: Thursday, 8 September 1864

Minds a flat; chalks on the corves; puts in the staples into the tubs, etc. Has been down 6 years. Was at the King Pit at Wreckington. There he found himself short of breath from the dust. Was often dizzy about a year or two back. Has whiles stood 24-hour shifts and once 36 hours here. Writes his name. Goes to night-school now and then. Goes to chapel often.

William Turner, aged fifteen, Seghill Colliery, 1841

Has been down pits 4 years. Has been lamed thrice in his leg. At the worst was off a fortnight. Once or twice has stood 24-hour shifts.

William Wood, aged thirteen, driver, Seghill Colliery, 1841

Has been down 6 years this pit. Was once off with sickness. Once he had his arm broken from the rolleys running over him. Once stood double shift of 24 hours. It is an easy place where he puts now.

Thomas Hedley, aged thirteen, Seghill Colliery, 1841

A postcard depicting Seghill Colliery in the nineteenth century. George Nairn collection

Seghill had opened in 1824 and had been purchased from the Carrs by Joseph Laycock in the late 1850s. There were usually about 500 workers at the pit but there had been a strike and at the time of the disaster about 400 worked. Naked lights were allowed in some areas but smoking was prohibited and there were caution signs placed at strategic areas as the pit was subject to blowers. The pit had been examined on the morning of the accident and pronounced safe by a master shifter with almost thirty-eight years experience. The deputies were responsible for locking the lamps and William Thompson, another with thirty-eight years in the collieries, had done this prior to the men descending. The explosion took place in an area where only safety lamps were allowed. Seven men and boys and eighteen horses were killed and a further eleven men and boys injured. Thomas Hogg, Robert Wood, Henry Mills and William Richardson were all older men and their condition was critical. It is possible that some or all later joined the list of the dead who were Thomas Heep, Richard Robinson and George Jackson who were all married. Those that were single were Henry Whitehead, John Mills, John Nieland and William Taylor.

The inquest was held at the Hope and Anchor public house at Seghill before deputy coroner Mr Cockcroft. On an inspection of the pit two lamps had been found unlocked and tobacco had been found in a jacket pocket although no pipe was discovered. The origin of the explosion could not pin-pointed with any certainty but it was thought that gas may have come from a fall in the goaf and ignited at one of the open lamps. The jury's verdict was based on that theory and a verdict of accidental death was given.

(27) Pit: Walker

Location: Walker, Northumberland
Type: Explosion
Fatalities: 8
Date: Monday, 24 October 1887

The pit fired shortly after 8pm when the majority of those working were shifters and stonemen. There were thirteen men working in the west district of the Brockwell seam, nine in the north district and an onsetter at the staple bottom. The Brockwell was the lowest seam at a depth of 204 fathoms (408 yards) and it was known that there was firedamp there and the adjoining strata which sometimes would come off in large volumes. Those in the west district felt the air-current change but other than that they were unaffected. They knew that this could be a signal that the pit had fired so headed to the north district. Meanwhile those on the bank had been alerted and organised an exploring party. Those already below and the explorers headed towards the north district but afterdamp impeded their progress for a time. Eventually they reached the seat of the explosion to find nine bodies lying within close proximity of each other. On closer inspection it was found that three of the men were still alive. They were quickly carried from the pit to receive medical attention. The bodies of the six dead men were then taken to bank. Two of the men that were rescued succumbed to their injuries. The injuries that William Hall had sustained were not too serious and he made a full recovery.

A memorial was erected in Walker cemetery to the eight men who lost their lives. Also included is a commemoration to John Dixon, aged 40, who died at the same pit on 29 August 1887 in similar circumstances.

The memorial to the eight men who were killed at Walker Colliery on 24 October 1887. Durham Mining Museum

The eight disaster victims were:

Anthony Hogg, 25, stoneman, married, child
Robert Laverick Wilson, 28, stoneman
James McMullen, 31, stoneman, married, family
William Richardson, 36, stoneman
Henry Defty, 36, shifter
John Hilton, 27, stoneman, married, child
Joseph Cockburn, 40, stoneman, married
John Pickard, 56, master shifter, married, family

At the inquest witnesses gave evidence as to complaints from the men on the slackness of the air and the consequent high temperatures. These conditions had been there for some days before the explosion but no gas had been detected. James Willis, Mines Inspector, came to the conclusion was that a shot had been fired and the powder gas projected from the shot raised a cloud of dust from the floor into the air containing some firedamp and that the flame from the shot had ignited the mixture. The expansion from this had raised more coal dust and the flame had extended in all directions until arrested by a falling quantity of coal dust in the wagon way and the returned flame had not passed the wet ground. The amount of firedamp in the air at the time the shot was fired was probably harmless in itself and it was considered that the coal dust alone would have transmitted the flame.

The panel on the Walker memorial listing the names of the eight victims who died in 1887 and also the name of John Dixon who died in a similar incident on 29 August 1887. Durham Mining Museum

The manager, Mr White, had just taken on the position a short time before. The colliery had been without a manager for some time as the man who had held the post had died suddenly. Willis had added that there was more work to do than officials to do it and this gave rise to a disinclination to listen and a disinclination to remedy sources of complaint from the workmen. Whether Willis was aiming his comment at the new and perhaps inexperienced manager or at all the officials the outcome of the inquest was accidental death.

(28) Pit: St Helen's

Location: Workington, Cumberland
Type: Explosion
Fatalities: 30
Date: Thursday, 19 April 1888

St Helen's Colliery was situated to the north of the town of Workington close to the sea shore and in 1888 employed around 230 men. On the morning of the disaster at about 9am a section of the workings had been set alight when a shot was fired. A party of thirty men were sent down to wall off that section. They worked throughout the day and came up for some refreshment at about 6pm. Just after the group descended again at about 8pm those on the bank heard a loud explosion which shook all the buildings at the pit-top. The managers had been in the office discussing the fire when the pit fired. They looked out of the window to see dense clouds of smoke issuing from the pit-mouth. When the smoke cleared they shouted down the shaft but there was no reply. On drawing up the cage it was to find it held a badly burned man who died a few minutes later. By this time a crowd had gathered and there was no shortage of volunteers to help those still below. By 11pm a number of the dead and injured had been brought to bank. Ten of these men were alive when brought from the pit but three died at the pit-head and two the following day at the infirmary the other five appear to have survived. The exploring party were suffering from the effects of the afterdamp and were said to be 'reeling like drunken men'. The worst sufferer was John Johnson, manager of the pit, who was himself carried from the mine on a stretcher. His brother William had also been involved in this first exploration and he stated:

We have been to the far end of the big dip, quite 300 yards away. We came across some bodies in the far end of the dip. We shook them, and left no means untried to find if any were alive, but all were dead. There were, as far as we could tell, 10 or 12 bodies lying all near together; there might be more. It was impossible for anyone to be alive who was in that part of the mine when the explosion occurred. It was when we were returning that we were overcome. My brother fell off the stretcher as we were bringing him along. All our party are safe now; the air is quite good where they are. There will be no trouble in getting them all to bank. Dr Ormrod, who had rendered gallant service

This image of Doctor Terrace at Bedlington is typical of the housing that mine-workers and their families lived in. The rain water butts and the privies opposite the houses showed that the sanitation certainly left something to be desired. George Nairn Collection

by accompanying the search party and returning to the surface with each of the rescued, said that the afterdamp was so oppressive that it would be impossible for anyone to go down for the other bodies.

It was obvious that the explosion had been far-reaching as one man was found in the engine-house and two at the bottom of the shaft. One of these men had been killed by the electric wire near the shaft winding itself around his neck causing strangulation. With the fire still burning and gas accumulating there was a high risk that there would be a second explosion so the recovery operation had to be called off. A good supply of water was obtained and work commenced to flood the mine to extinguish the fire. This accomplished on 30 April a team of eight men went down and sent up two more bodies. Those who still remained in the pit were underwater and would need to be recovered by divers. Twelve horses had also perished.

Recovered on 19 April:

John Ballantine (54), lampman
Robert Laybourn (22), shiftman
Wiggan Beaty (24), shifter
Richard Jackson (27), shiftman
William Gowan (28), whipper-in
JP Smith (35), joiner
Joseph Robinson (37), onsetter
Robert Hodgson (39), hewer
Joseph Stephenson (42), deputy
George Wright (42), shiftman
Joseph Iredale (44), shiftman
James Moffat (53), joiner
John Martin (58), shiftman
Recovered on 30 April:
Henry Nicholson (22), engineman
William Peel (47), deputy
Recovered by divers on 15 May:
James Hogg (31), hewer
Thomas Marrs (32), shiftman
Recovered on 21 July:
Thomas Hannah (25), shiftman

Recovered on 22 July:
Thompson Moore (25), whipper-in
John Williams (31), hewer
Isaac Gaskin (42), shiftman
Recovered on 29 July:
John Johnson (26), shiftman
Recovered on 30 July:
William Dixon (23), shiftman
Recovered on 31 July:
John Davidson (53) under-manager

Recovered on 1 August:

John Nicholson (34), hewer
William Banton (37), hewer
Robert Townsley (39), hewer

Recovered on 2 August:

William Tunstall (41), deputy
William Holstead (45), shiftman
Launcelot Laybourn (48), shiftman

Because it would be some time before the water could be withdrawn and the remaining bodies recovered it was decided to continue with an inquest and a Mines Inspector's Report. The results were made available on 12 June 1888 which showed that there had been six reports of gas before the disaster but the flow of air was considered sufficient to dispel this. Many of the men had considered it would be dangerous to shot-fire. A deputy had fired the shot which had ignited a gas feeder and in turn set light to the face of the coal. Everyone was withdrawn from the pit except for thirty-five experienced men. It was suggested at the time that there was no need for such a number but it was thought that they could only work in short spells because of the extreme heat. The extra men would make it possible for them to work in relays. The stopping could only be built up if the thick smoke was driven back. This had been accomplished by changing the air current which was thought to have driven an accumulation of gas onto the fire and ignite to cause the explosion. The conclusion of the Mines Inspector's Report was as follows:

It was suggested at the inquest that the firing of the shot in such a neighbourhood and the means subsequently taken to cope with the fire were blameable, or at least errors of judgment. However this may be, the mining engineers and colliery managers were unanimous in their testimony that, under the circumstances, no fault was to be found with either procedure, and upon the evidence taken before the coroner I am of opinion that there is no case for a prosecution.

The official statement by the coal-owners as to the number of the families of the married men who were victims showed thirty-four as being dependant. A Workington Relief Fund was set up give financial support to the dependants with Sir Wilfred Lawson MP of London as one of the promoters. A letter was forwarded to him from the Polydore De Keyser, Lord Mayor of London 1887–88, which read:

I understand you are taking steps to bring relief to the widows and orphans of the colliers who lost their lives in the recent distressing accident at Workington, in West Cumberland. If so, I shall be glad if you will add a donation from me. At the same time, if you think that an announcement that I shall be very happy to receive and to forward to the local committee any donations which the charitable public may like to remit to the Mansion-house would aid the fund, you are quite at liberty to say so. I observe that the necessity for a relief fund is the greater, inasmuch as the Cumberland miners are not so far advanced in the measures for insuring against these accidents which are now in successful operation in other mining communities. Should this be the case, the recent accident may possibly draw attention to the desirability of initiating the Lancashire and Welsh miners in the steps they take by means of their unions and provident funds to mitigate the distress when such sudden calamities arise.

This was not the last time there were to be multiple fatalities at this colliery due to shot-firing. The St Helen's Colliery and Brickworks Company Limited acquired the colliery in 1921 during the national stoppage. There were originally two mines, the No 2 Pit and the No 3 Pit, but owing to the stoppage, the lower seams at No 2 Pit were flooded and were not reopened with the upper seam abandoned. By 1922 there were 1,623 persons employed at the colliery of which 619 were in the mine at the time of this explosion which took place at about noon on Monday, 27 November of that year.

The inquiry was conducted by Thomas H Mottram, mines inspector, and the inquest heard before the coroner, Colonel DJ Mason. Both were held concurrently in the St Michael's Parish Room at Workington. The conclusions and verdict were that a shot fired by James Johnstone had caused the ignition of firedamp which had taken his life and that of five of his co-workers, namely:

John Davidson, 14, pony driver
George Davidson, 48, hewer, father of George
Graham Featherstone, 24, hewer

Many of these pit-ponies were killed along with their masters in mining accidents. Author's collection

Robert Nicholson, 29, hewer
James Johnstone, 34, deputy (died 28 November)
George Davidson, 20, hewer, son of George (died 30 November)

An overman, Fell, had felt a rush of wind and dust which he knew signalled an explosion. After taking some panic-stricken boys down to the bottom of No 3 Brake, and getting some canvas doors open to clear the brake of dust, Fell proceeded to search for survivors and came across Robert Nicholson and George Davidson, junior, who were seriously injured. He placed them in the charge of two other workers, Richard Edwards and R Thomasson, and then, after failing in an attempt to get into the affected area because of foul air, he retraced his steps down and entered by the level below, having by this time secured the assistance of William McMaster, a coal hewer, and another worker named Thwaites. Together they proceeded into Davidson's place from the intake side and found James Johnstone the deputy. He was placed in fresh air under the charge of McMaster and Thwaites, while Fell went for further assistance. He succeeded in organising two teams of four people each, one entering by Wilkinson's Level and the other by Ditchburn's Level (in which the air had become clearer) where they recovered three bodies.

It was recommended by both the coroner and the jury that the efforts of those involved in the rescue attempts should not go unnoticed.

Part Four

The Twentieth Century – and Still They Die

1910–1951

(29) Pit: Wellington

Location: Whitehaven, Cumberland
Type: Explosion
Fatalities: 137
Date: Wednesday, 11 May 1910

Wellington Pit had been sunk in 1840 by the Earl of Lonsdale's colliery agent with the first large accident taking place in 1863 but on that occasion there were no casualties. A fire had broken out which had resulted in the pit being sealed and the shaft flooded. It took five years before the fire was completely extinguished. By 1910 the pit employed over 500 men and was the property of the Whitehaven Colliery Company with the royalties still owned by the Earl of Lonsdale.

There were three shafts, a coal-drawing shaft, an upcast shaft and a water or pumping shaft. The coal that was worked was the Main Band and was about 10 feet thick. A haulage road extended from the shaft for about four miles due west under the sea and had a dip of about an inch to the yard. There were no horses in the colliery and the tubs were trailed by the workmen to the brakes or headings and from there by mechanical means to the shaft. The average output of coal was up to 1,000 tons per day. Under the Coal Mines Regulation Act, miners were appointed to make inspections under General Rule 38. Inspections were made on four days towards the end of March 1910 when all was found to be in safe working order.

On 11 May, the night shift had gone into the pit to change with the back shift at about 6.30pm. After the first set of back shift men had left the second set of night shift descended but as they were leaving the bottom of the shaft they were given an indication that things were not right. They felt the air reverse and saw large clouds of dust behind them which usually signified an explosion so some returned to the shaft to contact those on the bank. At about 7.40pm the under-manager, James Henry, descended the pit to find out why no coal was being sent up. The men told him their concerns and said they had received no reply when they had tried to telephone to the pit-head. Henry took a workman, Daniel Benn, and they headed down the incline while the rest of the men resumed their normal duties. The two men left the bottom of the shaft at about 7.45pm to seek out the cause of the problem and came across Stephen Gregory and Joseph Walker lying unconscious on the incline. Henry and Benn later stated that they had spent a considerable amount of time

A postcard depicting Wellington Pit, Whitehaven. Note the row of miners' houses on the hill. George Nairn collection

reviving the two men and then with serious forebodings they continued along the incline where they met Jack Weir and Joseph Kenmore who told them there was a fire in the friction gear. Had it not been for the delay Henry was quite sure they would have been able to extinguish the flames but it was about 10.30pm when he got to within about 400 yards of the area, and although the fire was still relatively small, the wood was alight and he was unable to cope with it himself so had left the pit to summon assistance.

Weir and Kenmore had been working in the No 5 district when Weir's son had told them there was an unusual amount of dust coming up the brake. Shortly after this one of the joiners, William Robertson, came and told them to leave as something was wrong. All thirty-three workmen in the district assembled on the level and Hugh McAllister, the deputy, went through the ventilation doors to see if it was safe to leave by that route. On his return he informed the men that he had found it impossible to get out that was as there was smoke coming down the incline. He then started to lead them out through the return but after walking a considerable distance the atmosphere became so hot they were compelled to turn back. They reached their starting point in the No 5 level and McAllister again tried to go through the doors to the incline and failed. It was at this point that it was later found that two of the workmen had chalked the following message on the ventilation door: 'Can not go any further. William O'Pray, J Lucas'. Weir eventually suggested that if someone were to accompany him he would try to get through the smoke up the incline. Kenmore volunteered and this decision was to ultimately save their lives. They both started through the smoke, passing through debris that had been blown about on the roadway. They reached the friction gear and found a smouldering fire on the right-hand side and flames on the left.

Wellington Pit looking south from the north shore. The candlestick chimney on the right and Wellington Lodge are all that now remain. Haig Mining Museum

Further up the incline they came into fresh air but when they tried to return the way they had come to lead the others out the air was too thick and hot for them to do so. Instead they continued up the incline where they had met Benn and Henry at about 10pm.

Officials were now gathered to contemplate measures to adopt to divert the smoke and a rescue team made their way into the pit. Walker and Gregory, the two who had been revived earlier, were found about two miles from the shaft and, although exhausted, both recovered. About an hour later Weir and Kenmore were brought out and able to relate how they had managed to escape. They told their rescuers that all their comrades had been alive and had plenty of air when they had left them in the No 5 district and this sent renewed hope to the thousands of people who had congregated to wait for news. Weir and Kenmore, after resting for a few hours, returned to volunteer their assistance in the rescue attempts.

This is from *The Times*, 13 May 1910:

> The difficulties of the rescue party were enormous, and although intermittent communication was maintained with them, no satisfactory news could be delivered to the crowds which had assembled above ground. Mr. J. B. Atkinson, the Government Inspector from Newcastle, arrived at 3 o'clock in the afternoon, and the managers of the pit were summoned to confer with him. A little while later it became known that there was between 15 and 16 hours' work before there was any prospect of ascertaining what chances there were of saving life. Additional appliances for extinguishing fire were sent down the pit, and by this time the rescue parties numbered more than 100 men, including some of the most experienced colliery experts in the country. The approaches to the pit were thronged by the wives and families and friends of the imprisoned miners, and most of the women, who had remained without food all day, declined, even when it grew dark and cold, to leave the spot although the reports from the officials offered no hope of further news. The managers of the mines and the engineers did all they could to cheer the anxious crowds in circumstances which provided little material for encouragement, and they delivered to them the many messages of sympathy, including that from the King, which arrived during the day.

Relatives and friends wait for news at the Wellington Pit after the disaster on 11 May 1910. The flag is at half mast as King Edward had died just five days before. Haig Mining Museum

Although numerous volunteers and officials made repeated attempts to try to reach the entombed men none of the various methods that were used to try to penetrate the workings through the smoke and tremendous heat met with any success. It was decided that there was a high risk of a further explosion so it would be prudent to withdraw the rescue party and wait for expert help to arrive. At about 11pm the following night-trained rescue teams from Armstrong, Whitworth and Co of Elswick and the Sheffield Mining Company arrived with specialist breathing apparatus. Two of the men, John Thorne and Henry Littlewood, from the Sheffield Company, were considered the best in their field. The gear that they carried could keep someone alive for an hour from even the most deadly gas. A team was put together consisting of the new arrivals, colliery officials and the most experienced miners. By about 11.30pm they had reached the bottom of the shaft and Thorne and Littlewood went ahead to check the air. After proceeding about 170 yards the smoke became so thick that they could not even see their torches and the heat was so intense that their exposed skin began to blister. Having no choice they turned back and reluctantly the party left the pit. After much consultation and expert opinion being put forward it was decided that those underground could not have survived the dense atmosphere and would by now have suffocated. The decision was taken by John Atkinson, Inspector of Mines, and the other officials concerned to seal up the workings which would starve the fire of oxygen so it would burn itself out. This course of action was vehemently disputed by many of the miners and the families of the victims as it was thought that some of those trapped could still be alive. Thirty-two and a half hours after the explosion the stopping was completed in the

Miners throng the road to the Wellington Pit after the explosion in 1910. 137 youths and men became victims of the worst disaster ever to take place in Cumbria. Haig Mining Museum

main roadway. The comrades of those entombed were not willing to give up without a fight and a party of miners went before the magistrate to request the demolition of the brickwork stopping so further rescue attempts could be made. A telegram was also despatched to Winston Churchill, the Home Secretary, requesting the same but permission was denied. On Sunday morning a party of seven made an effort to reach the fire via the return airway but again they were stopped by the thick smoke and intense heat. Further stoppings were then built in the return and in the intake. The mine, still with its human occupants, was completely sealed.

It was to be the end of September of 1910 when the mine was finally reopened. Heavy falls impeded progress so the last bodies were not recovered from their underground tomb until the beginning of October. One can only imagine the emotions of the victims' families during those months while they waited to lay their men-folk to rest. Identification of the badly decomposed bodies was a gruelling and, in some cases, an almost impossible task. At least one man was later found to have been buried in the wrong grave which would cause further grief to the family as to some religion was extremely important and they would have wanted the correct service read over their loved ones. Many families lost more than one of their menfolk with a total of seven from the McAllister family. This was the worst disaster to ever take place in Cumberland with the loss of the following 137 men and boys, identified as:

George M Ritson, 15, son of George
George M Ritson, 47, married, father of George
Robert Garroway, 15
John Garroway, 32
Alex Garroway, 37, married
James McCormick, 15, son of James
James McCormick, 58, married, father of James
Alex D McLaughlin, 16
Henry Rogan, 16
Thomas O'Hara, 16
William John O'Hara, 26, married
John McAllister, 16

James McAllister, 17
John McAllister, 21, married
Henry McAllister, 22
Edward McAllister, 23, married
Thomas McAllister, 44, married
Hugh McAllister, 49, married
James Ferryman, 17
Matthew Welsh, 17
Isaac Welsh, 20
James Southward, 18
Edward Toner, 18
James Smith, 18
Robert Smith, 18
George Smith, 38, married
William Walker, 18, son of William
William Walker, 37, married, father of William
Joseph Henry Walker, 27, married
William Walker, 32, married
Ralph Walker, 44, married
John Davy, 20
Edward Denver, 20
Thomas Wren, 20
John Wren, 37, married
Isaac Wren, 50, married
Henry O'Pray, 20
Joseph O'Pray
William O'Pray, 35, married
William Wilson, 21
Jonathan Wilson, married
John William Dunn, 21
James Irving, 21
William Irving, 45
George Boyd, 21
Daniel Branch, 21
Robert Wear, 21
Patrick Conner, 21, married
John Conner, 43, married
James McClusky, 21, married, son of Henry
Henry McClusky, 26, married, son of Henry
Henry McClusky, 55, married, father of Henry and James
John Brannon, 22, married
Thomas Brannon, 25, married
George Brannon, 49, married
Richard Cooper, 22, married
Robert Cooper, 29, married
Joseph Mossop, 22
John Anderson, 23, married

John James Vaughan, 23, married
Joseph Vaughan, married
Joseph Farrah, 23
John Mullings, 23
Thomas Reid, 23, married
Joseph Reid, 25, married
John Reid, 26, married, son of John
John Reid, 47, married, father of John
Joseph Reid, 55, married
William H Robertson, 25, married
William Mitchell, 25
James O'Conner, 25, married
Edward Butler, 36, married
Joseph Butler, 26, married
Edward Lynn, 26
Thomas Kenmore, 27, married
James Kennedy, 27
Dan Lewthwaite, 27, married
John McGarry, 27
Thomas McGarry, 31, married
James McGarry, 44, married
Anthony Corkhill, 28, married
Benjamin Cowie, 28, married
Joseph Heslop, 28, married
Christopher F Heslop, 30, married
John William Heslop, 34, married
James M Taggert, 28, married
John B Taggert, 39
William John Kelly, 29, married
Andrew Tinnion, 29
Thomas McCourt, 29
Thomas McCourt, 29, married, brother to Robert and James
Robert McCourt, 34, married, brother to Thomas and James
James McCourt, 36, married, brother to Thomas and Robert
William Chris Bell, 30, married
James Riley, 31
James Taylor, 31
James Moore, 31, married
Henry Moore, 45, married
Joseph Stephenson, 32, married
Fred Stephenson, 32, married
Arthur Trainor, 33
Jonathan Usher, 33, married
William Todhunter, 33, married
William Benson, 33, married
William Benson, 51, married
Jacob Glaister, 33, married

Thomas Joyce, 33, married
John Joyce, 35, married
John Dalton Lucas, 34
John James Lucas, 54, married
Alfred Brocklebank, 34, married
Edward Nicholson, 34, married
Joseph McQuillam, 34, married
James McGee, 34, married
Peter Greenan, 34, married
Henry Glave, 35, married
James McBain, 35, married
Edward O'Fee, 35, married
George McCumisky, 36, married
Michael McCumisky, 41, married
Alexander Gregg, 36, married
Mark Fisher, 36, married
William Henderson, 36, married
Thomas O'Neill, 38 married
William Elliot, 39, married
Henry Harrison, 39, married
John Harrison, 41, married
John Arthur Finn, 41, married
Robert Johnstone, 41, married
Joseph Fidler, 42, married
James McMullen, 44, married
James Roney, 46, married
John Hutchinson, 51, married
George Armstrong, 27, married
John Armstrong, 36, married
William Mullholland, 64, married
John Wright, 66

The bodies of Henry McClusky and his two sons were found in each others arms lying on a make-shift bed of brattice cloth. Besides the message chalked on the ventilation door by William O'Pray and John Lucas various others were found. One merely stated:

God is our refuge and our help.

Another, signed by James Moore read:

All's well in this airway at 4 o'clock. Thirty-five men and boys.

There was no indication whether the message was written at four in the morning or four in the afternoon so no one will ever know for certain if these men and boys were still alive and hoping for rescue when the mine was sealed.

A complaint was made against James Kier Hardie, leader of the Labour Party, as to a statement he had made referring to the disaster in which he said that he believed the miners were still alive when the stoppings were erected. Winston Churchill had said that this was 'a very cruel and a very disgraceful statement to make'. He added that he greatly regretted that a member of the House of Commons should have given currency to such a cruel aspersion. Hardie replied to this by saying:

> Winston Churchill's statement is evidently based on a very much abbreviated report of what I said. I give it as my opinion, based upon my practical experience as a miner, that at the time it was decided to wall up the mine, the miners were in all probability, still alive. The fire which imprisoned the miners, took place in what is known as 'The Bottleneck' and apparently this was the only means of egress from the workings. Beyond the Bottleneck the workings branch off in five main levels, and it would have been an easy matter to have had a safety road laid from these to the pit shaft, so that in the event of the main haulage road between the shaft and the Bottleneck getting blocked up, the other would have been available for the men to escape by. I suggested that these were matters which would require to be investigated and it is this suggestion which the Home Secretary characterises as 'cruel and disgraceful'. The working miners of the country will have a very different opinion. I hope Mr Churchill is not more concerned about shielding the mine owner than he is about finding out the truth.

On 2 December 1910, the official inquiry into the disaster concluded with no blame attributed to the owners or officials of the colliery. The coroner, Edward Atter, requested that the jury considered the steps taken with regard to the sealing of the pit. This was a matter which had caused great concern to the public as a Member of Parliament had gone out of his way to make the statement that the pit was closed for improper purposes. The jury must determine whether in the circumstances the closing of the mine was a rightful act. He thought there had been a certain amount of laxity regarding the observance of rules respecting the inspections of gas and the reporting of gas when found, but he did not believe there had been any criminal or wrongful neglect on the part of anybody. The jury found that the disaster was caused by an explosion of gas and coal dust combined that had occurred in No. 3 district and there was not sufficient evidence to show whether it was due to a defective safety lamp. They also found that the closing of the pit was a rightful and expedient act and

The long agonising wait at Wellington Pit to find out if their loved ones have survived the explosion. Haig Mining Museum

that no other means than those adopted could have been taken to reach the entombed men past the friction gear. No negligence or responsibility for the men's deaths could be attributable to anybody as there was no proof that the explosion was due to any non-observance of any statutory obligation and that due and sufficient care and all reasonable precautions had been taken for the safety of the men in Nos. 3, 5, and 6 districts.

The jury added recommendations that a proper register of names of men descending the pit at the different shifts should be kept; that a book should be kept specially for recording any withdrawals of men from working places on account of gas; that all reports of gas should be recorded; that the ventilation of the pit be made more adequate; that the watering of the main roadways by means of the spray be brought into operation; that the doors of the return air-way have special keys provided for the opening of the doors by the return side of the air-way; that there be a company of men trained for rescue and ambulance men; that the necessary appliances be provided and that a strict observance of the special rules by all officials be enforced.

The conclusion of the report of the Mines Inspector, RAS Redmayne, was that, although there was insufficient evidence to show the exact location, an explosion had occurred in the No 3 north district which was initiated by firedamp and carried by coal dust. All the bodies found in that area had died from a direct result of an explosion whereas those in the No 5 and No 6 districts had suffocated. Various recommendations were made towards providing a safer environment in the future. It was also stated that the decision to seal the workings had been the only alternative available. His report on the ventilation was as follows:

I am of the opinion that the ventilation of the working face was inadequate for the needs of the mine, having in view the gassy nature of the coal. I think that this inadequacy was largely due to the excessive leakage from the air current in its course from the shaft to the working face, and not to any want of ventilating power at the surface, any increase of which would not have materially affected the face ventilation. Further, that this leakage was due to errors on the part of a former management, and that the present management had made considerable efforts to improve matters, which efforts were being continued at the time of the explosion. This inadequacy cannot in my view, therefore, be wholly attributed to the existing management. Nevertheless the system of ventilating the 5th North district with 6th North air was an instance of bad mining practice and pointed to a want of proper appreciation of the dangers attendant on such a practice.

On 22 July 1910, the *London Gazette* published a list of the men who were awarded gallantry medals:

On the 11th May, 1910, a terrible fire occurred in the Wellington Pit, Whitehaven, at a point about 4,500 yards from the shafts. Various rescue parties, with great courage and self-devotion and at considerable risk, descended the mine and endeavoured to extinguish the fire and penetrate to the persons in the workings beyond the same. Thorne and Littlewood, fitted with breathing apparatus, reached within a distance of 150 yards of the fire, but were driven back by the great heat and effusion of gases. The others got to within about 300 yards of the fire, working in the smoke backing from the fire. It was found impossible to penetrate to the scene of the fire or to rescue any of the entombed miners. Had an explosion occurred – a by no means unlikely eventuality, seeing that the mine is a very gassy one – they would undoubtedly all have been killed.

John Henry Thorne was awarded a bar to the Edward Medal of the First Class that he already held and James Littlewood was awarded the Edward Medal of the First Class. The following men received the Edward Medal of the Second Class:

Wellington Pit employees:

Richard Walker Moore, mining engineer
Robert Richmond Blair, engineer and assistant general manager
Robert Steel, manager
Samuel Turner, manager
James Henry, under-manager
John Whillans, deputy
William Campbell, deputy
Thomas Swinburne, deputy
James Couthard, deputy
David Devine, deputy
John Wilson, deputy
Matthew Wilson, deputy
John Pearson, deputy
John Quale, deputy
John Graham, overman
Thomas Graham, overman
Daniel Benn, rope splicer
James Wren, rope splicer
William James Mullholland, hewer
James Dunlop, master wasteman
William John Henry, master shifter
John Fearon, shiftman
Matthew Walsh, shiftman
James Knox, shiftman
William Ball, shiftman
Charles Gibson, driftman
William Hoskin, driftman
Christopher Gregory, fireman
Robert McDonald, fireman
John Thomas Mather, collier and pit delegate
John Henry Parker, under-manager (Ladysmith Pit)
John Batty, overman (Ladysmith Pit)
James Taylor, deputy (Ladysmith Pit)
John Smith, overman (Ladysmith Pit)
Thomas Cannon, deputy (William Pit)
James McKenzie, deputy (William Pit)
Samuel Birnie, deputy (William Pit)
John Graham, deputy (William Pit)
John Rothery, overman (William Pit)
Wilson Graham, overman (William Pit)
Adam McKee, deputy (William Pit)
Ernest William Oswald, shiftman (William Pit)

Isaac Graham, shiftman (William Pit)
Joseph Lucas, hewer (William Pit)
Archibald Thom, manager (Moresby Colliery)
Thomas Banks, under-manager (Moresby Colliery)
Andrew Millar, manager (Lowca Colliery)
John Hanlon, miner's agent
Dr Charles Joshua Joseph Harris, colliery doctor

On 22 February 1911 the *London Gazette* published a list of additional names of men who also received the Edward Medal of the Second Class for their conspicuous bravery in the rescue attempt:

Fletcher Young
Edward McKenzie, senior
Edward McKenzie, junior
George Henry
James Scawcroft
John McAllister
William Ginbey
Thomas Birkett
Thomas Donald
Joseph Cowen
Hugh McKenzie
Allinson Mathers
John Hampson
Thomas Ferryman

By 7 June 1910, contributions from the public had reached £50,000 to assist the many widows and fatherless children left behind to mourn their terrible loss.

(30) Pit: Brayton Domain

Location: Aspatria, Cumberland
Type: Explosion
Fatalities: 7
Date: Monday, 26 April 1915

Although this was not a disaster on a major scale, because of the circumstances it warrants a mention. Two officials – a deputy and a shot-firer – not having the abilities equal to their responsibilities, seven men suffered a lingering and painful death.

The colliery was situated about seventeen miles NE of Whitehaven and in total employed just over 1,000 persons but at the time of the accident only eight were at work in the district which had been inspected twice by a deputy who found nothing to forecast danger. The explosion took place at about 11am with the subsequent Mines Inspector's Report by John RR Wilson detailing the cause:

The seam in the district concerned is 4-feet thick, and it has a strong blue shale roof. The method of working was bord and pillar. The pillars were being extracted alongside a 10-feet downthrow fault against which the goaf had been laid for some years.

This goaf was left to the rise so that any gas which was given off would rise into the goaf. The roof was so strong that no falls occurred in some cases for three months after the timber had been withdrawn. Adjoining the pillar in the course of being extracted there was an open area of at least 700 square yards. No gas had ever been reported in the district, but it had been found in other districts of the same seam. A 4-yard lift was being taken off a pillar, and the coal at the face of the lift was undercut on the loose side right through to an old bord, and on the fast side to within 6 inches of the old bord. Into this thin rib a slightly rising shot-hole was drilled until it penetrated the roof, and this at a point where a break extended vertically through the coal and into the roof for 20 inches to a horizontal parting in the stone which communicated with an open space above a fall in the old bord. This was a most likely place for gas to accumulate. It was gathered from the only survivor that a charge of gelignite explosive was fired in this shot-hole, and immediately there was an explosion in the old bord which communicated with the goaf adjoining it. There were practically no indications of violence resulting from the explosion, but there was evidence of flame and heat for a distance of some 180 yards from the point of origin. Coal dust apparently played a very subsidiary part, as fortunately, the mine was quite damp; otherwise the consequences would have been much more disastrous.

The points to be specially noted in connection with this accident are (1) that the attempt to blast down a rib of coal which was almost entirely undermined should not have been allowed; (2) that a powerful explosive like gelignite was most unsuitable for the purpose; (3) the discipline of the mine should have prevented a shot being fired next to a goaf the condition of which was unknown.

The inquest took place before the coroner for West Cumberland, E Atter, with the jury returning a verdict that the death of the seven men was caused by burns following an explosion. They recommended that 'no shot should be fired in a rib next to a goaf unless the rib could be examined from the goaf side'.

Of the eight men working in the vicinity of the explosion only Thomas Harris survived. He had been hit on the head and shoulder by a falling stone which had rendered him unconscious. The other seven men were terribly burned and must have been in unimaginable pain until death ended their suffering. Three of the victims were married and the Wilkinsons were father and son:

Robert Lightfoot, aged 20, died 28 April
Henry Wilkinson, aged 32, died 29 April
Thomas Birney, aged 64, died 2 May
Paul Rayson, aged 25, died 3 May
Thomas Herbert Little, aged 29, died 3 May
James Wilkinson, aged 59, died 21 May

(31) Pit: Woodhorn

Location: Woodhorn, Northumberland
Type: Explosion
Fatalities: 13
Date: Sunday, 13 August 1916

At this time about 2,500 miners were employed at Woodhorn Colliery which was owned by the Ashington Coal Company. As with the explosion at Brayton Domain this disaster could have been avoided if the officials had carried out their duties more responsibly.

At about 6am, in the Low Main Seam, the master-shifter instructed a repairing team to proceed to the Main Seam for the purpose of setting steel girders as roof supports. As the work was of a special nature the shift was composed of eight deputies and five other persons to assist them. The Main Seam was ventilated by fresh air entering the top of the drift from the High Main Seam and returning down the drift, to the shaft at the Low Main Seam. About thirty minutes after the team had left to head up the drift the master-shifter became aware that all was not right so he and others followed in the team's footsteps. In the drift below the Main Seam workings they found two men alive but unconscious. They were hurriedly carried out of the pit but both were to die without recovering consciousness. The bodies of ten men were found in various positions and the body of the thirteenth man, John Patterson, was found the following day.

Two of the men were found with broken necks lying against a girder. It was thought that one had stood on a tub to make preparations for setting a girder and had ignited a layer of firedamp near to the roof. One man had been severely burned and thrown for some distance. A man and a pony were also badly burned and covered by a roof fall with another four bodies showing signs of extreme force as well as burns.

Naked lights were used in this seam as gas had never been found and it appeared that a series of events had led to the disastrous outcome which was described in the Mines Inspector's report of which the following are extracts:

> On the date in question the air compressor was not at work (it was regularly stopped every other weekend from 5am on Saturday to 6am on Sunday), and further owing to shortness of steam, due to the fact that four stokers had failed to attend their work, the ventilating fan was running at a slower speed than usual. The compressed air being off, there would be no current of air passing into each heading beyond the last stenton.

The impressive memorial which now stands at Woodhorn Colliery Museum was dedicated in 1923 to those that lost their lives at Woodhorn Colliery in 1916. Durham Mining Museum

On the previous day, too, the fan had been off for repairs for six hours, and a furnace which would not give the same amount of ventilation had been lighted in its stead. It is interesting to note also, though we have it upon high scientific authority that a change of pressure will not effect the exudation of gas from solid coal that for the week ending the 13th August the barometer had steadily fallen .75 of an inch.

The roof of these main levels was supported by 12-feet girders, some 2 feet apart, resting upon running timbers each of which carried four girders, and a prop upon a footing was set beneath each girder. Along the east heading a fall, 4 feet in thickness and for a length of 90 yards, had taken place. The same witness offered the opinion that the fall of roof came away so suddenly that the air displaced by it had sufficient force to throw men to the ground and break their necks, also that the fall either liberated gas or was helped down by the pressure of gas behind it, and the gas ultimately became ignited.

Gas had never been seen in this seam and, therefore, it is likely that none of the eight officials made a very close search for it. I think it is certain that these officials never raised their lamps as high as their heads.

The inquest was held over three days at the end of which the jury returned the verdict:

That the deceased men were accidentally killed on the 13th day of August, 1916, while working in Woodhorn Colliery, by an explosion of gas in the Main Seam, and that such gas had accumulated through want of sufficient ventilation, and exploded through

The plaque at the base of the Woodhorn disaster memorial commemorating the names of the thirteen victims. The rear plaque depicts a colliery scene. Durham Mining Museum

contact with a naked light and before any fall of stone took place. The jury are of opinion that the management should see in future that written reports should be made for every shift, special or otherwise. The jury are also of opinion that there has been a certain amount of laxity on the part of the management for not seeing that sufficient ventilation was being maintained.

Legal proceedings which were instituted against the manager and engine-wright were dismissed by the Justices.

All but two of the victims were married and between them left thirty-eight children without a father:

John George Patterson, 21
Joseph Harrowgate, 29
Joseph Hodgson, 38, married
Daniel Harrison, 38, married
Walter Hughes, 38, married, four children
George R Hudson, 38, married, two children
David Armstrong 38, married, six children
Thomas Armstrong, 43, married, two children
George Marshall, 43, married
Ralph Howard, 44, married, five children
George Blair, 46, married, five children
Robert Hindmarsh, 46, married, three children
Edward Walton, 48, married, seven children

Walter Hughes had only returned to work at the colliery the previous week from spending some time in hospital after being gassed in the trenches. At the time of the disaster many of the men from the colliery were away fighting in the War.

Woodhorn Colliery was worked from 1894 until its closure in 1981. In 1989, the site was reopened as a museum which is recognised as the best surviving example of its kind from the North-East regional tradition.

(32) Pit: Haig

Location: Whitehaven, Cumberland
Type: Explosion
Fatalities: 39
Date: Tuesday, 5 September 1922

Whitehaven Colliery, which had been owned by the Whitehaven Colliery Company from 1913, had four pits known as the Wellington, William, Ladysmith and Haig. The latter employed 245 persons and all four mines were under the same agent and works manager, Robert Steel. The workmen were provided with a numbered token and unless this was produced, no lamp was issued to him without written authority from the manager. When starting work each man handed in his token at the lamp cabin and a lamp bearing the same number was issued to him. When they came to the surface after completing the shift they

Haig Colliery where thirty-nine men lost their lives in 1922. Haig Mining Museum

handed the lamps back and the tokens were given to them. In case of accident this served to identify anyone who might be missing. No naked lights were allowed in the mine, even in the downcast shaft. The only flame lamps in use were those carried by the officials making inspections.

There were six deputies who carried out the necessary inspections. The pit was divided into two districts, the North and South-West. Two deputies worked each of the three shifts and also an authorised shot-firer whose hours overlapped the day and backshift. On 24 August, one of the deputies went on holiday which left two deputies to cover his shift between them. They were both working twelve hours and not the eight hours fixed by the Coal Mines Act (1919).

Small quantities of gas had been found in the North District on separate occasions from July 1922 and, as was the procedure, these three areas had been fenced off. William Weightman, who was one of the deputies working overtime, had checked the pit on the evening of 4 September and found no gas in those areas or elsewhere. On the morning of 5 September there were eighty-two men in the pit of which thirty-nine were in the North District. At about 9am the banksman noticed a cloud of dust coming from the downcast shaft. He immediately sent word to Steel who in turn called for the Mines Rescue. Steel, Mr Brodie, manager of the William Pit, and George Cooke, Inspector of Mines, made their way to the Haig.

Meanwhile, in the pit, Alexander Millar, undermanager and another man had been standing near to the compressor house when they were knocked from their feet by a blast coming from the North District. The second man suffered broken ribs and other quite severe injuries but Millar managed to get to his feet and head inbye where he came upon the body of Thomas Telford. When Steel, his party and others descended they heard Millar calling for help and dragged him, almost unconscious, to safety. The pit was full of afterdamp and Millar had been affected. Steel and Brodie were also overcome and were taken to the local hospital for treatment. Those in the South-West District realised there had been an explosion and had made their way out of the pit. It was concluded that no one in the North District could have survived so it was decided that no further attempt could be made to penetrate the workings until the atmosphere could be sorted out.

The *Whitehaven Herald,* reported the following, on 6 September:

This closer view of the colliery shows the ambulances lined up in readiness. Haig Mining Museum

No pen-picture can ever hope to bring home to those who have not experienced it, what real warfare means, and no pen picture can visualise the scenes at the pit head following a big disaster. The latter is infinitely worse than warfare. Women with children in their arms and little hands clinging to their skirts wait with steadfast patience for possible news of the bread winner, and those around, who realise that all are doomed, dare not tell. Possibly the worst scenes of all, ensue during the identification of the bodies of the deceased. On Tuesday night, in some instances, men were not available for this purpose and women were ushered into the outbuilding of the pit, where the bodies were being made as presentable as possible, to pronounce the dreaded 'yes' or 'no'. Twice within a decade has Whitehaven experienced pit disasters on a large scale, and the stoicism of its colliery workers & their families, has been brought into bold relief.

It was to be 10 September before all thirty-nine bodies were recovered as it took time to restore the air current to a safe level and there were heavy falls which impeded the explorers' progress.

Referring to Thwaiteville, where some of the victims lived in ex-army huts, the *Whitehaven Herald* informed its readers that:

Probably the most tragic case is that of the deaths of George McCreadie and his two sons, Robert and Gordon. All lived in the same hut in Thwaiteville and even in the war, no wife sustained such a crushing blow in a single day. The widow is left with five children.

George, Robert Routledge, and Gordon McCreadie aged forty-seven, nineteen and seventeen respectively were father and sons. The other thirty-six victims were:

Thomas Parker Telford, 19
Jackson Sparks, 19
William John Sparks, 23, married
Albert Powe, 19
Thomas McDowell, 19

Robert McDowell, 44
Douglas James Michael Fell, 20
Robert Denwood, 21
Moses Huddleston Tyson, 24
Bernard Murphy, 24
John Moore, 25
Thomas Moore, 29
Joseph Moore, 29
William Hope, 25
Isaac Osbourne, 26
George Stevenson Parker, 26, married
William Carter, 26
John Bennett, 26
Leonard Ixon Hellon, 27, married
Samuel Coulter, 28, married
Thomas Henry Cooper, 28
Thomas Robinson, 29
William Weightman, 32, married

This image depicts the bodies being recovered from the No 4 shaft at Haig Pit. They were then taken to the cellars below the Power House which served as a temporary mortuary. The majority of the bodies were laid out with just their faces exposed for the purpose of identification. Haig Mining Museum

John Kirkpatrick, 32
Henry Goulding, 32
Sylvester McAvoy, 34
John Pattinson, 36, married, five children
Thomas Haig, 37
John Casson, 37
George Watson, 37
Albert Shepard, 39, married
Thomas Gilhooley, 39
John Carston Brewster, 39
James Graves, 46
Thomas Corlett, 58
Richard Denvir, 58

The bodies were laid out in the cellar below the power house at the colliery while an inquiry was held concurrently with the inquest. Smoking paraphernalia had been found but was ruled out as the cause, as were the lamps, none of which were found to be faulty. It was eventually concluded that the explosion had been caused by a shot being fired igniting firedamp and then propagated by coal-dust even though the area had been damped down. Thomas H Mottram, who compiled the Mines Inspector's Report, stated that he thought that a twelve-hour shift was too long for a deputy to work underground over a period of consecutive working days, and since the deputy, Weightman, had been on duty close on twelve hours, there was a question as to whether he was still fit to carry out the important duties assigned to him.

The jury made various recommendations with which Mottram concurred, the inspector stating:

The term 'wet throughout' relating to stone dusting should be defined and the Inspector thought the point should be referred to the Safety in Mines Research Board; The question of installing safety lamps in places where electric lamps are in use has been the subject of much controversy among mining men. The problem was some time ago referred to the Miners' Lamps Committee who have taken much evidence on the point and will shortly issue their report. There should be a spare deputy on each shift, that no deputy should be allowed to work overtime and that there should be greater inducements to men to take up the position of deputy; as far as the Haig Pit was concerned, no explosive should be used to get coal. Another issue that was mentioned was that no special system to check for prohibited articles had been approved by the Inspector and the onsetter conducted the search of about eighty men in fifteen minutes. There were grave doubts as to the thoroughness of this perfunctory method. During the course of the inquiry it emerged that matches and tobacco had been found underground and the jury thought it fit to recommend a stricter method of searching the workers for contraband.

A Mayor's Relief Fund for the families of the victim's was quickly put in place and, by 11 September, contributions amounted to a little over £4,000.

(33) Pit: Montagu Main

Location: Scotswood, Northumberland
Type: Inundation
Fatalities: 38
Date: Friday, 13 March 1925

Montagu Main had two shafts which were known as the Caroline and the View pits. The Caroline worked the Beaumont, Tilley, Five Quarter and Brockwell seams and the View worked the Tilley and the Brockwell seams; and it was in the Brockwell seam that the disaster occurred.

William Benson and Son, Limited were the lessees. The leasehold was immediately next to that of William Cochran Carr and both were in the Benwell Estate and held by the same landlord, the Brockwell seam extending through both leases. To 1848, when it was abandoned, Brockwell was worked by Matthew Liddell from a shaft on the leasehold of William Carr. Over a period it had been known as the Paradise, Beaumont or West Benwell Pit and was a mile and a quarter to the east of the View Pit. After transactions in 1876–7, the mineral field was divided and from December 1883 Thomas Walter Benson, William Robert Benson and Walter Benson leased an area of 750 acres. The Bensons were all dead by 1925 but they were the founders of Benson and Son Limited. The late William Carr became the lessee of minerals, including the Brockwell seam, to the east of the same line under a lease dated 23 October 1884. Both these old leases made no mention of the old workings. The old pre-1848 workings in the Brockwell seam from the Paradise Pit were never reopened and remained waterlogged. Their existence was known to William Carr and barred off on a line drawn on a working plan and the Brockwell seam was worked on another part of the lease from the Charlotte Pit which was some distance to the north of the Paradise Pit. On the western lease, the Montagu Colliery, from 1884 onwards, worked the Brockwell extensively from the View Pit and at the time of the accident the workings to the east had approached to within ninety-four yards of their neighbour's leasehold. They were required to leave a barrier of forty yards on their side of the boundary and so they had fifty-four yards to work.

An order form from the 1850s for the purchase of Benwell coal which includes the name of William Cochran Carr. Author's collection

Bord and pillar work had been in progress in the Brockwell seam from the View Pit in an easterly direction for some time. On the night of Friday, 27 March, two men had been working in this flat until 11pm after which the area was left idle over the weekend.

Joseph Robson, the deputy in charge of the district, made his inspection about 4.45am on Monday before the morning shift of 107 men and forty-one boys descended to the Brockwell. Small quantities of water had accumulated where the bord and pillar work was being carried out and Robson gave orders that it should be removed in the usual way. Four men, including Matthew Errington, began work in the area and shot-firing continued to bring down some coal and roughly straighten the face. Errington then sent a putter, James Tracy, to fetch Robson as there was a trickle of water coming from the face. On investigation Robson did not think there was any pressure behind but the water had a strange and unpleasant smell. He sent a boy to fetch an overman but just as the messenger left there was a loud bang. Robson told his son, also James, and Tracy to run. As he followed them he turned and saw water filling the tunnel. Two drivers, Tracy and young Robson coupled up some tubs and were drawn to the main road by a pony. Robson went into another flat and brought out five men. Eight men who were working where the water came in had no chance of escape and would have drowned very quickly. As the flow headed for the lower workings, it was seen by some workers who were able to warn their comrades of the fast approaching danger. Unfortunately enroute there was a depression and this quickly filled with water right to the roof. The majority of those who escaped waded through several feet of water but seventeen were trapped on the other side with no way out. Their bodies were later found huddled together appearing as though they had suffocated before the water reached them. A further thirteen had drowned in the lower districts in the early stages of

Montague Pit, Scotswood, the scene of a disaster in 1925. Thirty-eight men were to lose their lives when water inundated the pit. George Nairn Collection

The memorial that stands in Elswick Cemetery, Newcastle dedicated to the thirty-eight victims of the Montagu Pit disaster. Durham Mining Museum. Inset: *The plaque at the base of the memorial listing the names of the victims.* Durham Mining Museum

the inundation. Sam Evans, an overman, had gone back to try to help the men but had been caught on the other side of the fast-rising water.

Amongst the fire and rescue brigades that attended were those from Houghton, Ashington and Elswick. They soon had to withdraw because of the foul air becoming extremely dangerous.

Immediately after the inundation, G Spence, consulting engineer, gave this statement:

I am afraid it must be told that there is no hope. Nothing short of a miracle could give us back any of these poor men and boys alive. We have come up against poisonous gases where the only possible chance was. We have had telegrams from various people asking why we did not send the divers in. That was a physical impossibility. If there had been any possibility at all, we would have had divers at once.

Work also had to be stopped in the Caroline Pit which threw about 1,500 men out of work.

The inquiry was held at the Assize Court at Newcastle-on-Tyne in January 1926 before the Right Honourable Hugh Pattison Macmillan, with the assistance of Henry Walker, Chief Inspector of Mines, as the technical assessor. It was established beyond doubt that the cause of the accident was the breaking of the 'jud' (piece of coal, ready to be taken down) by the two shots causing the barrier between the old workings to break. It was estimated that the water pressure was eighty pounds per square inch and that after the shots had been fired, there was just six inches of coal holding it back. This slender barrier held the water for about half an hour. It was also established that no one in the mine knew of the danger. There was a general knowledge of the waterlogged workings of the old, disused Paradise Pit. Mr Carr said that his late father had once casually observed in conversation that borings should be done in that part of the workings but the inquiry did not put much store in this hearsay evidence.

On investigation it was found that were plans of the old workings in existence. There was provision made by the 1872 Coal Mines Regulation Act to preserve plans of abandoned mines. Further legislation followed in 1887 and 1896 but this made the plans accessible only to the inspectors and persons who the department had given a licence and the point in this disaster was that neither the lessors nor the lessees of the Montagu Colliery had access to the plans. Macmillan made recommendations that in future this legislation should change to avoid further disasters such as this.

Thirty-two of the thirty-eight victims were buried in a disaster plot in Elswick Cemetery where a memorial marks the site. A Garden of Remembrance was created in the grounds of St Margaret's church in Scotswood in 2006, with funding of £25,000 from the SITA Trust.

The deceased were:

Fred Armstrong (37)
William Halliday (47)
John Murthwaite (27)
John Martin (48)
Matthew H Errington (53)
James Nixon (29) son of Joseph
Joseph Nixon (55) father of James
Thomas Danskin (20)
Charles Simpson (49)
Isaac Booth (40)

Robert Thompson (56)
John Thompson (58)
William Thompson (56)
William James Johnson
Frederick Thomas Dent (25)
Thomas William Batey (42), brother to Christopher
Robert Heslop Batey (54)
Ralph Carr (32)
Robert Havelock (40)
William Armstrong Trewick (32)
John Thomas Trewick (30)
William Alnwick Fowler (34)
John William Lee (56)
Samuel George Evans (52)
William Armitage Lyons (21)
Alexander Learmouth (21)
James Steele (21)
Richard Rogers (21)
William Guthrie (22)
Thomas Alfred Latcham (14)
David Griffin Dixon (17)
Charles Edward Gray (24)
John William Potts (23)
John Charles Salmon (17)
John Robert Fitzpatrick (19)
Matthew Hetherington (28)
George Gill Hetherington (32)
Edward Jackson (39)
Christopher Batey (44), brother to Thomas

James Steele's brother-in-law, John Dodd, was later also killed on 7 July 1929 by a fall of stone.

In April 1927, an inrush of water in the Caroline Pit at Montagu Colliery caused the death of David Armstrong. The manager and undermanager were fined £10 each for not examining some disused workings and making sure they were free of water. Their defence was that they had no plans relating to these workings and so did not know of the danger.

(34) Pit: Edward

Location: Wallsend, Northumberland
Type: Explosion
Fatalities: 5
Date: Sunday, 9 August 1925

It has long been established that many of the fatal accidents in coal mines were avoidable had safety measures been in place and care and attention been instrumented. There were few, especially in the early years of the industry, where an inquiry laid blame squarely on the coal-owners or mine officials' shoulders. The inquiry into the explosion that took place in the Edward Pit in 1925 did apportion blame. In that year there were 1,092 persons employed at the pit which was part of the Wallsend Colliery. The last recorded disaster at Wallsend had been ninety years previously (1835) when eleven perished. On this occasion five men were killed: Francis Matthews, aged 18; Reginald Hogg, 21; Joseph Coxon, 32; Peter Banks, 49; and John George Young, 27. Four died as a result of burns and shock and the fifth of carbon monoxide poisoning. One other man was injured and many were affected by the poisonous air but had all recovered.

Electric safety lamps were in general use at the colliery and each leading machine-man also carried a flame safety lamp. At the time of the explosion three electric chain machines were in use at the Yard Seam in the 9th West District. There were two small faults in the district, and No 1 machine was opening out a face on the rise side of the last one proved. No one had been at work between 1pm and midnight on Saturday when a shift descended to clear cut coal in front of the machines and to prepare the face. No inspection was made of the district before work commenced, which was in contravention of Sections 63 and 64 of the Coal Mines Act (1911).

An overman descended at 4am on Sunday morning to see that the faces were clear for the coal-cutting machine men who followed at 6am. This official admitted at the inquest that he only travelled to the front of No 1 machine, and did not make any inspection of the face to the right of the machine and towards the fault. After leaving this machine, he lost the light in his oil flame lamp and shortly afterwards lost another light which he had procured. He proceeded to complete his inspection with an electric lamp, which was useless for gas detection. Men who had been at work from midnight to 6am between Nos 1 and 4 machines were all using electric lamps and later said they noticed nothing unusual in the

The new colliery at Wallsend which was completed about 1911. George Nairn collection

atmosphere and heard no falls of roof. No unusual conditions as to roof weighting or disturbance of the ventilating system could be traced prior to the explosion; in fact the roof in the neighbourhood of No 1 machine was still standing a fortnight after the explosion.

There were twenty-three men on the 6pm shift, including three sets of machine-men. On the way inbye, Joseph Coxon, who was to work No 1 machine, told Lauder, who was to have charge of No 4 machine, that he had knocked out his oil flame lamp, and there was evidence of this lamp having been re-lit. The last person to see the four machine-men alive was a driller named Mayne, who was drilling in the first gateway to the left of the second south mothergate. About fifteen minutes before the explosion he went to the No 1 machine to get assistance to remove a full tub, and saw Coxon at work at the running machine. Mayne's description of the condition of No 1 machine face was that 'it was pretty warm'. After receiving assistance in removing the tub he commenced drilling and shortly afterwards he felt a rush of hot air and dust from the direction of No 1 machine. Then, without cutting off the air from his drill, he made his way outbye and was later rescued in the second south mothergate by a machine-man named Turner. Later Turner stated that he had noticed a rush of air and thought it was due to a big fall of roof. On going out to the landing he found the main separation sheet between intake and return on the ninth west engine plane blown down and also noticed a smell of burning. He had all the switches for the coal cutter circuits opened and at about 7.20am ran to the shaft to telephone the lamp man on the surface to the effect that 'something' had happened in the ninth west district.

Although rescue work was carried on courageously by the personal efforts of the workmen and officials and all persons who took part deserved praise, the Central Rescue Station was not notified until more than two hours after the explosion, and even after this loss of valuable time there was complete lack of direction on the part of the management, with the result that effective work by the rescue brigades did not commence at the advanced base until 11.15am, nearly four and a half hours after the explosion occurred. If anyone had survived the explosion this delay would have ensured that rescue would have been too late. It was also pointed out that because of the lack of direction and knowledge on how to conduct a rescue some of those that tried unnecessarily risked their lives, and in several cases had themselves to be rescued.

The possible sources of ignition which were scrutinised were flame safety lamps, matches, abrasive sparking of the cutter picks, and electricity. In the entire absence of other evidence the investigation of this explosion pointed to the conclusion that an accumulation of firedamp was ignited, probably by electrical arcing at the plug connector on No 1 machine; that the limitations were fixed by the volume of the explosive atmosphere, and that coal dust took practically no part in the explosion. No inspection of the district was made before the midnight shift commenced work. The overman failed to make an inspection of the face between No 1 machine and the fault and it was thought unlikely that he had made an examination for firedamp anywhere in the district. There seems little doubt that he lost his light on two occasions due to the presence of firedamp. It was stated without hesitation that the laxity of the officials in neglecting to make proper inspections and tests for firedamp was the primary cause of the disaster. The investigation also showed that no effective use was made of the flame lamps supplied to the machine-men. They only had very vague ideas as to where to make tests for firedamp. It was generally admitted that the flame lamp was hung at the gate-end switch on arrival at the commencement of the shift, and allowed to remain there.

On 16 March 1926, at Wallsend, Charles Nelson, agent of the Wallsend and Hebburn Coal Company, and Edward Nutley, manager of the Edward Pit, were charged, on four dates, with failing to inspect part of the mine in which workmen had to pass; with failing to make a full and accurate report of inspection; with failing to keep a report of the inspection; and with failing to keep a report at the mine. Nutley was also charged on four counts with failing to assign their proper duties to officials. Gas would have been detected if an examination had been made. The Mines Department took a serious view of breaches of the 1911 Act in view of explosions, and had circulated all collieries strictly to comply with the regulations, especially on Sundays, when few men were working.

(35) Pit: Haig

Location: Whitehaven, Cumberland
Type: Explosion
Fatalities: 13
Date: Sunday, 12 February 1928

At 10.15pm on 13 December 1927, the afternoon shift had already left and the night shift were on their way in to the workings when there was an explosion. Four men were killed but had this taken place just a short time earlier or later the death toll could have been catastrophic. Rescue brigades were called and on reaching the seat of the explosion, two and a half miles under the sea, they recovered the bodies of two deputies: James Fitzsimmons and James Knox. Extensive falls made the exploration tough going but a little later the body of William Bradley was recovered. A fire was then found to have taken hold in the No 3 district and despite hours of exhausting work it could not be brought under control. It was decided that the only way to extinguish the fire was by sealing the area off to starve the flames of oxygen. This left the body of Harold JG Horricks still lying somewhere underground. Both the Haig Pit and the Wellington were closed throwing almost 2,000 men out of work.

The men returned to work at the Wellington Pit at the beginning of January but the Haig remained closed with over a thousand men still idle. By February 1928 the indications pointed to the fire being extinguished so work commenced to break the seals and remove the stoppings. On 11 February, a party of twenty-four men, including officials and two rescue teams, entered the mine carrying canaries to test the air. The birds seemed unaffected so the men continued forward. One of the rescue teams, wearing breathing apparatus, went in to where a fire was known to have broken out. They returned to report that it was out and the area cool. At about 11pm some of the men returned to the surface for rest and refreshment with food and drink conveyed down to the remainder and breathing apparatus recharged. At just before midnight work was resumed with five deputies left to clear up the falls in the road and the rest of the group, led by Robert Steel, continuing in search of the body of Horrocks. Further progress was made when just at midnight there was a series of three explosions. The third was violent with the men being thrown from their feet and foul air filling the area. Eleven men groped their way for about three miles in the blackness to the shaft bottom by using rails and telephone wires as guides. They were bruised but managed to reach safety. Three rescue teams immediately descended to search for survivors. The canaries that they carried quickly succumbed to the foul air and no further progress

Robert Steel (centre) pictured with two rescue workers. The shaft supports are made of wood which points to this photo having been taken at the Wellington Pit.
Haig Mining Museum

could be made when they came to the main stopping and found it completely wrecked with huge falls barring their way. The whole area was unstable and there was evidence that another fire had broken out. Bags of stone dust were used to seal the area and the teams withdrew in the certain knowledge that none of those that remained behind the stopping were alive when it was constructed.

In total the two events took the lives of seventeen men of whom all but two were married with one of these, Jesse Cresswell, engaged. The widow of James Rothery had already lost a brother, an uncle and five cousins in pit disasters. Many of the men left behind young children. The bodies of Harold Horricks and the following thirteen men were never recovered as No 3 district was not reopened and they remain in their tomb deep under the sea to this day.

The fatalities were as follows:

Jesse Cresswell, 29, Deputy
Frank Wilkinson, 32, Deputy
William Graham, 41, Deputy
James Rothery, 41, Deputy
Hugh McKenzie, 49, Deputy
George Hodgson, 56, Deputy
Henry C Hanlon, 30, Miners' Association Agent
Peter Burdess, 35, Sub-Inspector of Mines
John Tyson, 47, Colliery Officials' Association Secretary
William Loudon, 48, HM Junior Inspector of Mines
Robert Fell, 48, Under Manager
Robert Steel, 58, Agent and Works Manager
John T Walker, 38, Overman

The two deputies, Fitzsimmons and Knox, who were victims of the first explosion in December 1927, were heroes of the Wellington Pit disaster of 1910, with Knox being

This is one of the two headgears that were in use at the Haig Pit, the last deep coal mine worked in the Cumbrian coalfield. It has been preserved and is now an outstanding feature at the Haig Colliery Mining Museum. The author

awarded the King Edward Bronze Medal for his efforts. Both men had also played their part in the Haig Pit disaster of 1922. Robert Steel had also received the Edward Medal after the Wellington Pit disaster and had assisted in the rescues at the William Pit in 1907 and the Haig Pit in 1922.

An inquiry into the deaths was opened on 8 March but with no way of conducting a detailed inspection of the pit the cause could not be ascertained.

(36) Pit: Haig

Location: Whitehaven, Cumberland
Type: Explosion
Fatalities: 27
Date: Thursday, 29 January 1931

In less than ten years the toll of multiple fatalities at the Haig Pit had reached fifty-six and in January 1931 another twenty-seven lives were lost. It was 8.15 on a Thursday night when an explosion rocked the workings. Of the 169 men underground forty-five were in the No 3 District which adjoined that which had served as a graveyard for the previous victims.

The *Whitehaven Herald* described the initial rescue:

> About nine o'clock, an improvised rescue party, which included Mr Marron, the Manager of Haig Pit and Dr E. H. Ablett, and who were without respirators, descended the mine, and battling through enveloping clouds of dust and gas, penetrated to within a mile of the seat of the explosion. One of the first things they found was a small stationary engine which had been wrenched bodily from its foundations and hurled about forty yards. On top of it was the body of its driver. Altogether, seven men were rescued, as well as recovering three bodies. This, another magnificent piece of work, ended only when rescuers were in danger of losing consciousness. Never have I seen rescue men work to better effect. They were splendid, said an official who had experience of the three previous explosions at Haig Pit. The worse job was that of carrying out the bodies, some of which were in a terrible state.

Rescue teams were soon at the scene with their breathing apparatus enabling them to enter the badly damaged workings to restore ventilation and prevent the outbreak of any fires. Mr Marron continued to work with the rescue parties even though he had to be revived twice after suffering the effects of the suffocating gas. The force of the explosion had apparently reversed the air-current sweeping afterdamp down Jolly's Drift into the Wellington Pit. When the lights went out and breathing became difficult the men made their way to safety. Harry Stephenson, an overman, turned back to warn four miners who did not know of the danger. He tied a handkerchief over his mouth and, finding a man unconscious, tried to revive him but he himself lost consciousness. The rescue team were there in time to save Stephenson and two others but they were too late for John Ruddy and Thomas Quirk.

Huge crowds gathered around the pit awaiting the outcome, described on 5 February by the *Whitehaven Herald*:

> The scenes at the pit head were those irretrievably bound up with all big mining disasters. As the night advanced a crowd, growing rapidly every minute, made its way to the pit yard and divided into small knots, discussed the situation in hushed tones. The moon shone brilliantly through the frosty air, lending to the gloomy pit scaffolding, a touch of the mystical. All the offices were ablaze with light, telephone bells tinkled incessantly, busy workmen hurried to and fro. By half past nine, several hundreds of people had assembled chiefly wives, parents and intimate friends and relations of the entombed men. They bore the ordeal bravely, waiting patiently for news of their loved

Coal trucks which are on display outside Haig Colliery Museum. The author

ones. A large detachment of police had been rushed to the yard, but their task was an easy one – the crowd which had increased by half past ten, to close on a thousand, maintained perfect order. Some of the Whitehaven cinemas had flashed on the screen a slide bearing the announcement of the disaster. Large numbers of the audience left the buildings and made for the pit by bus and on foot. Women with shawls hurriedly thrown around them, some carrying babies, were also present at the pit, and the roads were thronged with folk.

It was not until the first survivors arrived at the surface that the psychology of the crowd changed. Inside the tiled chamber, at the pit head, a large crowd had assembled, and as the cage rose into the room to unload its precious contents, wives, parents, and friends made a rush in the hope of seeing their loved ones. Those who were fortunate enough to recognise the men, rushed to them and flung their arms around them, linked them, as they led them down the lonning into the pit yard, their eyes filled with tears and were widely hysterical with joy. As for the others, tears they had manfully withheld, commenced to flow, and with the arrival at the surface of the first mangled body, many women broke down completely and sobbed and were led away by relatives.

Margaret Mather stood at the pit-head for hours waiting for news of George Parker, who she was to marry within a few days. Instead of a wedding she would attend a funeral as her long wait ended with her betrothed's body the last to be recovered. George Parker and his father were two of the twenty-seven victims:

Joseph Henry Gainford, 18
John Bailey, 21
John Richardson, 21, son of James
James Richardson, 45, married, father of John
Robert Hewitson, 22
John Thomas Rogan, 22, married
Joseph Rogan, 49, married
Robert Groggins, 23
William Wilkinson, 24, married
Wilfred Hocking, 24, married
Joseph Smith, 27

The tub that was struck by the Cardox shell at the Haig Pit during shot firing. Haig Mining Museum

Matthew Storey, 28, married
Richard Hayton, 29, married
John Edward Slack, 30, married
George Parker, 31, son of George
George Parker, 58, widower, father of George
John Telford, 33, married
Edward Cockbain, 40, married
James Knox, 43, married
William Cowen, 47, married
Robert Vincent, 50, married
John Holliday, 50, married
Joseph Kelly, 51, married
Robert Parkin, 53, married
John Ruddy, 58, married
Thomas Quirk, 59, widower

Sir Henry Walker, HM Inspector of Mines, submitted a report in May 1931 as to the cause of the disaster. Gas had been detected on numerous occasions in the area and, on this occasion, had been ignited. It appeared that a shot fired had been unable to penetrate the coal and had rebounded and hit a steel tub. Walker's conclusions were that the ignition had been caused either by a spark within the exploder or across the conductors of the firing cable or sparks or heat caused by the friction of the Cardox cartridge when it struck and penetrated the end of the steel tub.

The two pits remained closed until 19 March as the miners refused to return to work until they were totally separated from each other. They also wanted the stoppings broken down and the fourteen bodies recovered. The management would not agree to these requests but did agree to ban shot-firing. In April, tests were carried out on improved Cardox shells which caused a walkout by the men. They returned to work only when the management guaranteed that shot-firing would not take place when the men were working.

(37) Pit: William

Location: Whitehaven, Cumberland
Type: Explosion
Fatalities: 12
Date: Tuesday, 3 June 1941

There were to be three explosions which claimed multiple victims in the William Pit throughout the twentieth century. The first of these was on Tuesday, 26 November 1907 when five men were killed and seven injured. Those who died were Joseph Kennedy and William Vincent Fitzsimmons, both aged 22; Jason Rowe, 24; Alfred Burns, 26; and William Hanlon, 30.

The cause of the explosion was found to be that shot-firing had taken place where inflammable gas was known to be present.

The second of the three explosions took place at about 2.15pm on Tuesday, 3 June 1941, taking twelve lives. The eight men who died in the pit and four who succumbed soon after from their injuries were:

James George (aged 18)
Robert McCreavy (20)
William Ernest Harker (21)
Sydney Barbour (21)
John Peter Burney (21)
James Wells (27)
James O'Pray (38)
Cornelius Moore (40)
Charles James Martin (41)
William Perry (50)
Robert Baxter (55)
Jonathan Curwen (57)

Eleven others were injured, some seriously, but all survived. They were: John R Baxter, William Benson, Thomas Dougherty, Joseph Fitzsimmons, Richard D Glaister, William J Kerr, Thomas McCormick, George Porthouse, Joseph Rogan, Henry Ruddick and Moses Stephens.

Preparations for the extension of the New Form stopping were going on and on 29 May a start was made to remove about five feet of flue dust packing from the outbye side of the wall. This work was interrupted by the Whitsuntide holidays and nothing more was done for a further three days. The work resumed on 3 June. About ten feet of the upper section of flue dust was still to be moved to each end of the brickwork and the face of the narrow cutting. Men were set to work and the fireman lent a hand from time to time. A B Dawson, who was in charge of the surveying and planning department of Whitehaven Collieries, arrived between 9 and 9.30am when the removal of the flue dust had been suspended while the passage was enlarged by taking the coal from the left hand side. Dawson went to the end of the cutting and cleared the flue dust up to the coal at the end of the cutting. The dust was warm but not hot and the temperature of the brickwork at this stage was said to have been normal. Later a connection was made to the water column and at about 12.20pm water was applied to the exposed surface of the flue dust close to the roof of the face of the cutting. The dust soon became saturated and the excess water went to where the old road had been crossed. It soaked through the dust there and disappeared and not trace of it could be found. This occurrence was referred to at the later inquiry. Shortly after the hosepipe had been put into position at 12.20pm the manager appeared and the general position was discussed, the other stoppings and surroundings inspected and at about 1.30pm the party consisting of Dawson, the manager, Mr Farquhar and the fireman, G Savage, withdrew after the workmen had already gone when their shift ended. The water was left running and the door in the New Front stopping was left open and those to the air lock were both closed with the outer door plastered round its edges. Most of the day shift had gone outbye and the afternoon shift had started work. Due to absenteeism which was to be expected after a holiday, some work on the day shift had not been completed and a few hands had stayed on for about an hour to catch up. They had completed their work about 2pm and gathered at the Lowca Junction to wait for the train to take them to the pit. The rope haulage was set in motion on the afternoon shift at 2.10pm. At about 2.15pm work in the Countess Bannock District was going on as normal. A number of men were near the Lowca Junction ready to ride outbye and some had already taken their places in the tubs while others were about to do so. Farquhar, Dawson and Savage were proceeding outbye on foot. These three had reached the Six Quarters Turn about half way to their destination when the explosion occurred. They felt a temporary reversal of the air current and realising there was a problem they retraced their steps. As they approached the Lowca Junction they saw wires down and props displaced. In the stopping area the doors of the airlock were gone and there was a hole in the brick partition through which smoke was issuing. Work to get the injured from the pit was put into operation with extreme speed and by 4pm everyone was out. By 9pm the eight bodies had also been recovered.

At the inquiry evidence was given that water gas could be produced by water being poured on red-hot coal. Firedamp was ruled out and it was thought that the gas was a chemical product of the action between water and the fiercely burning coal. The HM Inspector of Mines, FH Wynne, concluded his report by saying:

> As regards to deep-seated fires arising from other causes, care in the application of water is clearly called for where there is a possibility of the production of water gas. Within the limits of this report it is impossible to discuss or attempt to define the conditions which may give rise to the risk of water gas explosion and the precautions to be taken. It is, however, important that an attempt to do so should be made and to this end I recommend further investigation and perhaps research.

No blame was laid at anyone's door as this was considered an unusual and unforeseen circumstance.

(38) Pit: Harrington

Location: Workington, Cumberland
Type: Explosion
Fatalities: 15
Date: Monday, 9 December 1946

The Lowca Colliery had first been sunk in 1908 and was described as 'a big industrial sentinel' as it stood on a 500 feet hill overlooking the Solway Firth. In 1946, it was owned by the United Steel Companies Limited.

Lowca employed 770 persons of whom 530 worked underground with 210 men and thirty women working at the surface and until December 1946 there had been no serious accidents. On the day of the explosion there were 208 men below ground with fifty-three of these in the Main Band Seam which was 350 feet below sea level. The seam was regarded as a gassy one and during the six months prior to the explosion the statutory reports showed that firedamp had been detected in the No 2 District on several occasions but the reports were found to be incomplete, also no inspection on behalf of the workmen had been carried out during this period. The area was very wet with water raining in from the roof in the headings and it was decided to advance the number 2 and 3 headings which rose about one in eighteen, rapidly to the boundary which was fixed by a limiting minimum cover of 240 feet so as to drain the water from the area. When the thirls were no longer in use they were sealed off by using corrugated sheeting and brattice cloth. The undermanager stated that there was a shortage of both bricks and bricklayers and that was the reason why brick stoppings were not built. He considered the sheet metal both safe and effective.

On Monday, 9 December the morning shift started work in No 2 District at 5.30am. There were thirteen men accompanied by the deputy, Thomas Miller, a stone-worker, John McMullen and William Hoodless, an overman. McMullen was working at the transfer point a little way outbye when Miller came to speak to him at 8.30am; Miller then headed back inbye and had walked about fifteen yards when the pit fired. McMullen knew no more as he was knocked unconscious.

By 9.45am the first trained rescue team had arrived from the Brigham Rescue Station, under the direction of the Superintendent, Mr Charlton and with teams following from other collieries a total of twelve brigades in all took part in the rescue operations. The seat of the explosion was almost four miles inbye well under the Solway Firth. Everything possible was done to get into the affected area to give aid to the men there. It was soon evident that the explosion had travelled outbye to the transfer point on No 3 road with tremendous force. The air crossing which was a considerable structure, had been demolished, doors and other ventilation arrangements destroyed and there were numerous heavy falls. All this made the work of rescue very difficult and because of the wet conditions, very unpleasant but no effort was spared by officials or workmen from this and other collieries to reach the entombed men. McMullen was the lucky one as two men had assisted to get him some distance from the danger area before they were affected by the afterdamp and had to leave him. He was found soon after by a rescue team and, although he was burned on the left side of his face, his left thigh and right hand, he survived. Some of the men in other districts had been affected by the afterdamp and required treatment. The last body, which was that of Thomas Miller, was eventually recovered five days after the explosion. He had been buried under a fall and it took a considerable amount of time and manpower to remove the hundreds of tons of debris that covered him. The fifteen men in No 2 District were all killed leaving behind fourteen widows and thirty-three children. They were:

Charles Sharpe, 26, married, child
Robert Henry Brown, 31, married, child
Thomas Bird, 31, brother to John

John Wright Bird, 46, married, child, brother to Thomas
Ronald Pflaumer, 32, married
John Fox, 34, married, four children
Harrison Fidler, 37, married, two children
John Tolson Hill, 39, married
William Hoodless, 41, married, two children
Thomas Austel Miller, 41, married, two children
Wilfred Chapman, 42, married, two children
Daniel Largue, 43, married, two children
Thomas Addison, 44, married, child
Robert Maurice Bruney, 44, married, three children
William Henry Enis, 54, married, twelve children

As always there were individual personal tragedies besides the terrible loss of so many lives. William Enis was the father of twelve children, a large family by any standard. His youngest daughter Annie was aged only four. William Hoodless had just been elected to the Lowca Council. The local sports scene was badly affected with the Football Club losing many supporters. The two Bird brothers were on the Committee and Dan Largue was a county referee. Another brother, Harry, should have been at work that morning but had not felt too well and had stayed in bed. Charles Sharpe was a well known boxer and as well as having a young child his wife was pregnant. Thomas Miller had started work in the St Helens Colliery when he was fifteen years of age and after almost thirty years he was appointed as a deputy. During his life in the pits he had several near escapes. About twelve years previously a fall trapped his arm and it was feared that it would have to be amputated but he made a good and rapid recovery. Two weeks before the explosion he had sat an examination to train Bevin Boys. Robert Burney was a collector for the National Savings and was very fond of dancing while Robert Brown was the organist at the Lowca Methodist Church. He recently had completed a course on mining engineering and was related to the Birds.

The conclusion of the inquiry was that the men had met their deaths by an explosion of gas which had been ignited by William Hoodless unscrewing the top of his lamp. The gas was present because of inadequate ventilation which was due to a series of incidents. One of the statements made was:

All the cost cutting, corner cutting and shortages of skilled labour and Government Inspectors caused by the war were at last reaped in a bitter harvest.

Various recommendations were made by the Inspector of Mines, Sir John Felton, regarding improvements to ventilation, more skilled training and less cost-cutting and he finished with the following statement:

Tribute was justly paid by all parties at the Inquiry to the excellent work done by the Rescue Brigades and numerous others who voluntarily gave their services in an endeavour, unfortunately of no avail, to rescue the victims of the disaster and later to recover the bodies. These efforts were in accord with the well known high traditions of mining men and I gladly record thanks to all who thus served.

A fund set up for the families of the victims raised many thousands of pounds.

(39) Pit: William

Location: Whitehaven, Cumberland
Type: Explosion
Fatalities: 104
Date: Friday, 15 August 1947

This was the third explosion to take place in the William Pit in the twentieth century and by far the worst so far as loss of life was concerned. In 1816, the pit had been selected to test Sir Humphrey Davy's wonderful invention of the safety lamp and at that time was described as 'the most dangerous pit in the Kingdom'. In 1947 the pit had just come under the ownership of the National Coal Board and employed 440 persons.

It was about 5.50 on the evening of Friday, 15 August when the bell in the winding engine room began to continuously ring, a sound that foreboded trouble below as it was caused by crossed wires. No time was spared in organising rescue teams and volunteers were called for to assist on the surface. There were so many willing to help that the police had to turn some away. Within an hour 2,000 people had congregated as near to the pit mouth as they could get.

Everyone's worst fears were realized when it was announced that a violent explosion had ripped through the workings. To begin with there was some confusion as to how many men were underground but the number was soon established as 117. Ten men had been working away from the seat of the explosion on the side leading to the shaft bottom. Three were injured and the others made their way along the main road to the shaft to telephone for help. The injured men were got to the surface and the remaining seven stayed below to help with rescue.

The image depicts from left to right: James Weighman, aged 23, John Birkett, 50 and Daniel Hinde, 40. The men were described by the press as the 'three miracles' because of their escaping death after the explosion at the William Pit in 1947. Haig Mining Museum

The rescue teams had heavy falls and extremely dangerous conditions to deal with in their efforts to find survivors. Hope was fading when, twenty hours after the explosion, one of the teams saw three men coming towards them. At first it was thought they were members of one of the other teams but it was soon realised that they were men that had been thought lost. The three survivors had been in a drift between the falls and John Birkett, the oldest and most experienced of them, had managed to lead them to a place where there was fresh air. After some hours they decided they had better try to find a means of escape. After having to change direction many times because of the gas, with wet scarves over their faces, they managed to reach the main haulage road where they came upon the rescue team. The route they had taken was extremely unstable and it was considered a miracle they had reached safety without being gassed or crushed by a fall. Birkett, Daniel Hinde and James Weighman were taken to Whitehaven hospital to recuperate from their terrible ordeal. On their way out they had passed a group of about forty men, all in a crouched position, with no sign of life. Birkett expressed the opinion that there was little hope that there could be other survivors. To the waiting crowds, however, news that survivors had been found sent a message of renewed hope but this was soon dashed as more and more bodies were found, many of them in groups, some with their arms around one another and some who had obviously been crying as the tears had streaked the coal-dust on their faces.

A newspaper reporting on the 'miracle' of finding men alive and giving hope there would be others. Author's collection

Eventually there were only four men that remained undiscovered and it was thought their bodies must be hidden under heavy falls. At about midnight on Monday, the Gloucestershire RAF School for Police Dogs arrived bringing with them three Alsatians. One of the dogs was Jet who had received an award for finding fifty people trapped under debris during the London Blitz. He had been brought out of retirement to help in this 'search and find'. Once underground the dogs led the rescuers to a particular fall from where the last of the bodies was eventually recovered on Saturday, 23 August.

The gravediggers could not cope with the enormous task that had to be carried out but there were hundreds of volunteers to help in this final act for their relatives, friends and colleagues. The 104 men that perished were:

Ronald Hughes, 20
Harold John Carr, 22
William Ronald Musson, 22, married
Richard Musson, 36
William Telford McMullen, 22, married, young child
James McMullen, 27, married, two young children
William Williamson, 27, married, young child
John Henry Maddison, 22, married, two young children
Edward McAllister, 24, married, two young children, son of Isaac
Isaac McAllister, 54, married, two of eight children at home, father of Edward
Thomas Fox, 24
Joseph Fox, 37
William Lewis Pickering, 24, married, young child
William Pilkington, 66, married, four surviving children, father of John and Thomas
John Pilkington, 32, married, four young children, son of William, brother to Thomas
Thomas Pilkington, 27, son of William, brother to John
William Pilkington, 51, married
Richard Cartmell, 25
Adam Raby, 25, married
John Richard Mowat, 26, married, young child
James Clifford, 26, married, two young children
Samuel Devlin, 27, pregnant wife, two young children
William Johnson, 27, married, two young children
Thomas Lancaster, 27
William Harker Lee, 27, married
Richard Atkinson, 28, married, young child, brother-in-law to George Hutchinson
James Atkinson, 45, married, four children
Patrick Murtagh, 28, married, two young children
Lawrence HP Murtagh, 41, married, three children
James Rigg, 28, pregnant wife, young child
George Henry Wilson, 29, married, young child
Joseph Wilson, 38, married, two children
Matthew Wilson, 46
John Paragreen, 30, married
Dennis Lyons, 31
William Martin, 32, married, two young children

Edward Reuben Ray, 33, married, young child
Thomas Allan, 33, married, two young children
Henry Trohear Allan, 39, pregnant wife, two children, son of John
John Douglas Allan, 59, married, father of Henry
Joseph Gerald Diamond, 33, married, four children
William Nicholson, 33, married, young child
Sydney O'Fee, 34, married, three children
Henry Barker, 34, married, five children
James Murray Bowes, 34, married, three children
Wilfred Farrer, 34, married, two young children
Ralph Walker, 34, married, two young children
Hartley Byers, 35, pregnant wife, four children
Walter Wylie, 36, married, two children
James Murray, 36, married, four children
William Murray, 39, married, three young children
Thomas Thompson Smith, 36, married, three young children
Harold Smith, 41, married
Thomas Barnes Smith, 62, married, five children
Thomas A Nelson, 36, married, three young children
Leonard Seward, 36, married, two young children
Andrew Agnew, 36, married, two young children
Henry Gibson, 36, married, three young children
James William Lambert, 36, married, two young children
John Edward Moore, 37, married, three children
Joseph Moore, 39, pregnant wife, three children
James Moore, 63, married, four children
Jacob E Bridges, 37, married, three young children
John Nelson Garner, 37, married, two children
Vincent McSherry, 38, married, two children
William Foulder Grearson, 36, married, five children
Richard Edward Grearson, 47, married, six children
Ronald William Hewer, 38, married, four children, brother to Joseph
Joseph Wilson Hewer, 40, married, five children, brother to Ronald
Francis Murdock, 38, married, three young children
John Quirk, 38, married, two children
William Fisher, 39, married, four children
John Joseph Renwick, 39, married, two children
Robert Glosson Mulholland, 39, married, five children
Thomas J Shackley, 40
Albert Edward Saulters, 40, married, child
Herbert Calvin, 40, married, three children
James Cambell, 40, married, child
John Milburn, 40, married, three children
Albert E Salters, 40, married, child
George Johnstone, 41, married, three children
Joseph Norman, 41, married, three children
Albert Tweddle, 41, married

William Henry Crofts, 42, married, four children
Thomas Richardson, 42, married
Robert Conkey, 43, married, two children
George Hutchinson, 44, married, child, brother-in-law to Richard Atkinson
Henry Shilton, 44, married
Mark J Shaw, 45, married, seven children
Joseph Brannon, 45, married, three children
Thomas Brannon, 57, married, four children
William Clark, 46, married, child
Thomas Turner, 46, married, adult child
William Arnott Walby, 46, married
James Gibbons, 47
Joseph Banks Marshall, 47, widower, two children
Edward Glaister, 48, married, nine children
James Leeson, 48
John Anderson, 50, married, seven children
Thomas Gladstone Dixon, 55, married, three adult children
James Richardson Barwise, 49, married, two young children
John Henry Doran, 50, married, eight children
John Robbs, 56, married, nine children
George Porthouse, 54, married, adult children
Thomas Woodend, 64, married, adult children

One of Herbert Calvin's sons, James, was to later lose his life in the 1951 Easington Colliery disaster.

Forty-six witnesses, including the three 'miracle' survivors gave evidence at the inquiry. A published report on the findings stated:

Expert evidence was unanimous that the explosion was caused by the firing of an explosive placed in a shot-hole drilled in the roof and directed towards waste behind and immediately contiguous to the coal face. This shot-hole passed through a roof break, and was in contact with, or close to, a cavity containing inflammable gas which led to a larger accumulation of explosive gas in the inaccessible waste. It was evident that the shot-firer, who lost his life in the explosion, could not have examined the hole for breaks, and this was a grave omission.

Since the firing of shots in the roof in the waste at a longwall face is practised in many pits throughout the country, the report emphasizes the need to direct the immediate attention of managements at such collieries to the grave risks attending this practice in mines where inflammable gas is not unknown. We can no longer afford to run the risk attending the firing of shots in close proximity to any inaccessible wastes containing or likely to contain inflammable gas on the grounds that such places are inaccessible and cannot be examined by the flame of a safety lamp.

The National Coal Board, in answer to the findings of the inquiry, issued the following statement:

The impressive sculpture by Colin Telfer which is dedicated to the coal-mining history of the area is situated near the Beacon on Whitehaven Harbour. The plaque reads 'The end of an era. This monument was unveiled on Friday 17 June 2005 by Violet Wilson, former screen lass in celebration of the past, to inform the present and encourage the future'. The author

The NCB will give immediate and close attention to the preliminary report. Since they assumed control of the industry in January last the board and the divisional coal board have given high priority to the task of maintaining, and where possible improving, safety standards throughout the coalfields. They will continue to do all in their power to make the mines still safer and to eliminate avoidable risks.

A Relief Fund had been put in place and was to be closed at the end of February 1948. Between August 1947 and January 1948 the fund had accumulated £105,676. Food parcels had also been sent to the victims' families at Christmas.

(40) Pit: Weetslade

Location: Weetslade, Northumberland
Type: Explosion
Fatalities: 5
Date: Monday, 1 October 1951

Although not strictly termed as a disaster as this was the last incident in Northumberland or Cumberland to incur multiple fatalities it warrants inclusion. Weetslade adjoined Burradon Colliery with the workings connected but with separate systems of ventilation. There was no history of an explosion at the colliery but inflammable gas had been

The team of the Durham and Northumberland Fire and Rescue Brigade in an Armstrong Whitworth rescue car stationed at Elswick in about 1911. The men were specially trained in fire-fighting both above and below ground. George Nairn Collection

considered a hazard and safety lamps had always been used. In 1944, the conditions were considered suitable for complete mechanisation and caterpillar mounted Universal arcwall coal cutting machines, Joy loaders, shuttle cars and trunk belt conveyor system were introduced. All the equipment was driven by electricity. At 6.45am on a Monday, a workman, Vincent Love, felt a temporary reversal of the ventilation which raised some dust at the 3rd East intake. He could not understand what had happened so reported the incident to the overman, Thomas Short, and told him that he thought there had been a fall inbye. Short went about halfway down the 3rd East intake to investigate but did not find anything unusual. He went back along the return airway as far as the compressor stenton, into the intake and back to the 3rd East Junction and saw nothing untoward. Satisfied in his own mind that there was no cause for alarm, he went outbye to the Hopper to arrange the work for the oncoming shift. At 8am George Williams, a shot firer, spoke to Love at the 3rd East Junction and commented on the peculiar smell in the air when he reached the face. Love told him what he had experienced and added that the pumpman and four men who had been dismantling equipment had not been seen for a while. Williams spoke to Short on the telephone and received instructions to investigate. Accompanied by a workman, he travelled the intake to the overcast, three stentons back from the charging station, which he found severely damaged and beyond that discovered a heavy fall. The two men then went back to the compressor stenton and entered the return airway and after going inbye for 170 yards were driven back by foul air. They were joined by Short who brought with him some deputies from the incoming shift. They tried to explore the return airway but they were also driven back by the foul atmosphere. They confirmed that the overcast was wrecked and Short telephoned the surface to report that apparently the five men that had been in the district had been trapped behind a large fall which blocked the intake airway. The trapped men were in the Bensham Seam about 750 feet below the surface and just over a mile from the bottom of the shaft. When the manager was informed he descended the mine with the undermanager and travelled inbye by the intake. When they reached the booster fan they went into the return to see what conditions were like and realised by the state of the air that something more serious than a fall had taken place. The manager sent a message to the surface to call the Rescue Brigade and they went along the intake to the damaged air crossing where they found that repair work had already begun to try to restore the ventilation inbye. These repairs were almost complete when the rescue team arrived at 11.12am and it was only then that the true nature of the accident was revealed.

The first rescue team soon discovered that water in the return airway, outbye of the charging station, had risen to within two feet of the roof as the pump had been out of action for several hours. Progress on the intake side was prevented by a large fall but this was bypassed by means of the charging station and the return airway to the pumphouse where the body of the pump attendant was found. To reach the other missing men falls would have to be cleared and the ventilation restored. Before any such work could start, it was discovered that the water was rising at such a rate that the return would be blocked and all energies were directed to installing a pump in the main intake at the charging station. Before suitable pumps could be transported into the district, which took some hours, the water had reached the roof of the return roadway and cut off all ventilation which made the site of the pump untenable. A new site was selected and with great difficulty the pump was installed but it could do little but hold the water at the level it had reached. A larger pump was required and this could not be installed until nine days after the explosion. On 9 October the larger pump was started and the water was lowered to a foot below the roof of

Members of the Elswick rescue team in 1931–2. Front row: Smith, Arneil. Back row: Gibbons, Fawcett, Proctor, Knox, Smith, Harson, Coulshed. George Nairn collection

the return and air started to flow again into the explosion area. The rescue brigades had established that the air in that area was foul and knew that it was impossible for the missing men to have survived.

By 11 October ventilation was restored and rescue teams were sent in. They discovered that the entrances to the charging station had collapsed and falling girders had broken open batteries causing acid to spill. They also found that the charging batteries on the other side were undamaged and that the terminals were dangerously close to steel girders. Air samples were taken and found to contain firedamp so, confronted with an alarming situation, in which seventy or so men were facing imminent danger, it was deemed prudent to withdraw everyone from the mine until the situation could be properly assessed. It was decided that if the water was allowed to rise, this would dilute the acid and hopefully, discharge the undamaged batteries. It was estimated that ten days would be required for this and an extra two days were allowed as a safety margin. Plans were made to re-enter the district on the 23 October. On that date, the sandbag stoppings were breached and ventilation was established as far as the compressor stenton. The first stage of the recovery operation was now finished and the Rescue Brigade withdrew. The bodies were eventually recovered between 19 and 29 November. The five men that perished were: Matthew Charlton, aged 30, loader operator; John Fisher (33), driller; Thomas Patterson (54), timberman; Thomas Whitney (56), deputy; and John Davidson (58), pumpman.

At the inquiry it was found that no electrical equipment could be faulted. There was no contraband found in the clothing of the victims and there was no evidence of spontaneous combustion. Although a definite cause of the explosion was not ascertained, it is a fact that the only possible igniting medium found in the whole course of the protracted investigation was the fusion on the shuttle car battery. There was evidence that the explosion could only have occurred as a result of something done by the men in connection with the operations in which they were engaged near where their bodies were found. An open verdict was returned on those who lost their lives. In conclusion the Inspector of Mines, W Brown, stated:

I welcome the opportunity of recording in some detail my sincere appreciation of the assistance so willingly and ably given by the Weetslade miners who courageously and tenaciously performed miracles of work in some of the most trying conditions, even for a pit their representatives displayed great consideration and forbearance especially during moments of stress and strain from those directing the operations. The Rescue Brigades, comprising 199 teams of Permanent Corps men and colliery trained men from Northumberland and Durham, gave full cover underground during the emergency, frequently being the spearhead of the operations, during which 7,678lbs of liquid air were used in 50 sets of self-contained breathing apparatus.

Fifteen years later, in September 1966, Weetslade Colliery closed forever. The last colliery to close in Northumberland was Ellington in 2005 and the last in Cumberland was when the shafts of the Haig Pit were sealed in March 1986.

Glossary of Mining Terms

afterdamp	a lethal mixture of carbon monoxide and other gases that is produced following a firedamp or coal-dust explosion.
back-overman	has less responsibility than an overman.
bank	top of the pit.
banksman	person on the bank responsible for landing the workforce, coal and other materials.
blackdamp	a mixture of carbon dioxide and nitrogen. The term is also applied to an atmosphere depleted of oxygen, rather than having an excess of carbon dioxide.
bord	principal working place of four or five yards wide where one or two hewers would be employed in their task.
brattice	main division of a shaft or the partial slit in a workplace used to direct the air flow.
canny	North-Eastern dialect for something or someone good.
cage	a timber or metal compartment consisting of up to three platforms and used for the ascent or descent in a shaft of men and materials.
chargeman	the person in charge.
chock	a roof support made up of a number of blocks of wood.
choke/choak damp	also known as blackdamp, this is a colourless, odourless gas consisting of carbon dioxide and nitrogen.
Clanny	a safety lamp designed by William Clanny in 1869 and improved in the 1880s which was heavier but safer than the Davy.
collier	a skilled miner, also known as a hewer, who extracts coal from its situation using a wedge or pick.
corf/corves	strong wicker baskets used to convey the coal and men, the term later applied to tubs.
coupler	a boy who connects the tubs of coal to form a train.
cradle	open-sided lift used for maintenance to the shaft walls.
creep	a peculiar rise of the floor of the mine usually caused by the forcing of pillars into soft bottom by the weight of a strong roof.
Davy	a safety lamp invented in 1815 by Sir Humphrey Davy which was cheaper than the Geordie lamp and popular with the coal-owners.
deputy	a qualified official in charge and responsible for the immediate supervision of an underground district of a coal mine, including its safety, production, supplies etc – according to legal requirements.
downcast	a shaft which lets fresh air into the mine.
drifter	person employed in driving into rock other than coal.
driver	boys that draw the waggons from the crane to the shaft and drive the horses on the main underground road.
firedamp	explosive gas, especially methane, released from coal seams.
flat lad	boys employed in raising the corves of coals by the power of a crane from the trams onto a rolley or waggon.
furnaceman	a person that looks after the main ventilating furnace.

galloway	pit-pony or pit-horse.
Geordie lamp	name used in the North East dialect to describe a Stephenson safety lamp.
gin	a pit-head drum and rope machine, usually horse-drawn, used in early collieries for winding in the shaft; also known as a whin-gin
gin-rope	a rope used as part of the whin-gin.
goaf/goave/gob	those parts of the mine where all coal has been extracted and left a vacant waste area.
hagger	Cumberland local dialect term for a hewer.
hewer	see collier.
inbye	the underground area towards the coalface.
kibble	large iron cauldron or bucket.
landry-box	receptacle into which the water pumped from the mine is discharged.
marra or marrow	North-Eastern dialect for a work-mate or friend.
onsetter	a person who operates the shaft signals at the pit-bottom, communicating with the winder and banksman. In early pits he would also assist the loading of tubs/trams of coal onto the cage.
outbye	the underground area approaching the shaft bottom or mouth of a level.
overman	a senior official in charge of the workmen and is responsible for keeping an account of the overall condition and running of part of the mine.
pullie	see rolley.
putter	a person who fills the baskets or tubs and pushes them on trams to the crane or shaft.
pyrite	a mineral commonly known as fool's gold, when stuck against metal it produces sparks.
roadway	underground tunnel used to reach workplaces and through which air passes.
rolley/rolly	a small wagon that transported corves/tubs of coal also known as a pulley/pullie.
shifter	a person who repairs passageways and keeps them free from obstruction.
shot-firing	the use of explosives in stone drifts and mine workings.
staith	place where coals are shipped by a machine or spout.
stenton	a short heading at right angles to a cross-cut.
Stephenson	safety lamp invented in 1815 by George Stephenson which gave a brighter light than the Davy and was popular with the pitmen but was more expensive.
stith	see chokedamp
stoneman	a person who excavates any hard stone.
switch keeper	a boy who attended to the switches on underground railways.
thirl	a cross-hole or ventilation passage between two headings.
trapper	young boys or girls employed in opening and shutting the canvas flaps or doors for ventilation usually working alone and in the dark.
upcast	shaft (or type of chimney) from which the foul air escapes.
viewer	a manager or under manager of a colliery.
water leader	a boy who removed the water from horse-ways and other places.

Bibliography

Books

Sykes, John, *Local Records Volumes* or *Historical Register of Remarkable Events which have occurred in Northumberland and Durham, Newcastle-Upon-Tyne and Berwick-Upon Tweed.* Volumes I – II (John Sykes, Bookseller, 1833 & 1844)

Everett, James, *The Wall's End Miner* (Hamilton, Adams & Co; and J Mason, London, 1838)

Fordyce Thomas, *Local Records* or *Historical Register of Remarkable Events which have occurred in Northumberland and Durham, Newcastle-Upon-Tyne and Berwick-Upon Tweed.* Volumes III – IV (Thomas Fordyce, 1867 & 1876)

Hair, Thomas Henry, *Views of the Collieries in the Counties of Northumberland and Durham* (Newcastle-upon-Tyne, 1844)

Richardson, MA, *The Borderer's Table Book* or *Gatherings of the Local History and Romance of the English and Scottish Border.* Volumes I – VI (Henry G Bohn, London, 1846)

Richmond, Thomas, *Local Records of Stockton and the Neighbourhood* (William Robinson, Stockton, 1868)

Fynes, Richard, *History of Northumberland and Durham Miners,* 1873

Galloway, Robert Lindsay, *Annals of Coal Mining and the Coal Trade.* Volume I, 1898. Volume II, 1904

McCutcheon, John Elliott, *The Hartley Colliery Disaster, 1862* (E McCutcheon, County Durham, 1963)

Duckham, H & B, *Great Pit Disasters* (David and Charles, Newton Abbott, 1973)

Fryer, AG, *The Burradon Colliery Disaster 1860* (AGF Publications, Blyth, Northumberland, 1996)

Garraway, Amanda M, *104 Men* (Hayloft Publishing Ltd, Kirkby Stephen, Cumbria, 2007)

Reports

Atkinson, WN & JB. *Explosions in Coal Mines* (Andrew Reid Printing, Newcastle-upon-Tyne, 1886)

Evidence given to the *Children's Employment Commission, 1842*

Newspapers/Magazines

Durham County Advertiser
Gateshead Observer
Harpers Weekly
Liverpool Mercury
London Gazette
London Illustrated News
Northern Daily Mail
Penny Illustrated
South Durham and Cleveland Mercury
Sunderland Echo and Shipping Gazette

Stockton and Hartlepool Mercury
South Durham Herald and Stockton Journal
Sunderland News and Northern England Advertiser
The Graphic
The Guardian
The Times
Tyne Pilot
Whitehaven Herald

Internet
http://www.haigpit.com (Haig Colliery Mining Museum)
http://www.dmm.org.uk (Durham Mining Museum)
http://www.chmrc.co.uk (Coal Mining Resource Centre)

Index

O'Pray, William 151, 121
Ormrod, Dr 110
Ostle and Dunglinson 66

Parker, George 145
Railway Inn (Walker) 100
Ranson, Michael 61
Ravensworth, Lord 67
Reay, Mr 44
Redmayne, RSS 123
Reed, Stephen 48, 50, 58, 62, 73, 81–2, 95, 100, 105
Reid, T Wemyss 90
Richmond, Rev Leigh 25
Robertson, William 115
Robinson, Ralph 85
Robson, Joseph 135
Russell, William 12, 30

Scotswood 134–5, 137
Selkirk, John 15
Sharp, George 85
Sharp, William 85
Sheffield Mining Co 117
Shields Daily News 83
Shields, Major Harry 98
Shields, Margaret 88, 97
Shields, William 86, 88, 97–8
Short, John 85
Short, Thomas 158
Slaty Ford 16
Solway Firth 149
Spence, G 137
Steel, Robert 129–30, 142
Stevenson, George 20
St Helen's Colliery & Brickwork Co 112
Swallow, Mr 27
Sykes, John 29, 61

Telfer, Colin 156
Telford, Thomas 130
Thew, Elizabeth 26
Thew, George 25–6
Thew, John 26–7
Thew, William 25–6

Times 27, 59, 70, 78, 101, 116
Thomasson, R 113
Thompson, Robert 76
Thorne, John 117
Throckley 58
Thwaiteville 131
Top Row (Whitehaven) 37
Turnbull, George 104
Turnbull, Robert 86, 89
Turner, Joshua 102

Urwin, William 81

Victoria, Queen 96

Wales, John 67
Walker, Joseph 114, 116
Walker, Sir Henry 137, 146
Wallbottle 17
Wallsend 24, 29, 45, 57–8
Wallsend and Hebburn Coal Co 141
Watson, Thomas 84–5
Weatherly, Thomas 83
Weetslade 156
Weighman, James 151–2
Weir, Jack 115–6
Wellington Lodge 116
Wilkinson, David 86, 98
Williams, George 158
Willington 50, 60
Wilson, John RR 125
Wilson, JR 25
Wilson, Violet 156
Whinghill 41
Whitehaven 27, 33, 37, 58, 64, 114–5, 125, 144, 147, 156
Whitehaven Colliery Co 129
Whitehaven Herald 38, 41, 55, 130–1, 144
White, Mr 109
Whitley Bay 41
Willis, James 108
Woodhorn 127
Workington 51, 109, 112, 148
Workington Hall 54
Wynne, FH 148